ENTITLEMANIA

ENTITLEMANIA

How Not to Spoil Your Kids and
What to Do If You Have

RICHARD WATTS

GREENLEAF
BOOK GROUP PRESS

This publication is designed to provide accurate and authoritative information in regard to the subject matter covered. It is sold with the understanding that the publisher and author are not engaged in rendering professional services. If expert assistance is required, the services of a competent professional should be sought.

Published by Greenleaf Book Group Press
Austin, Texas
www.gbgpress.com

Distributed by Greenleaf Book Group

For ordering information or special discounts for bulk purchases, please contact Greenleaf Book Group at PO Box 91869, Austin, TX 78709, 512.891.6100.

Design and composition by Greenleaf Book Group and Kim Lance
Cover design by Greenleaf Book Group and Kim Lance
Broken Heart Lollipop © Stas Knop. Used under license from Shutterstock.com

Cataloging-in-Publication data is available.

Paperback ISBN: 978-1-62634-349-8

eBook ISBN: 978-1-62634-346-7

Hardcover ISBN: 978-1-62634-345-0

Part of the Tree Neutral® program, which offsets the number of trees consumed in the production and printing of this book by taking proactive steps, such as planting trees in direct proportion to the number of trees used: www.treeneutral.com

TreeNeutral

Printed in the United States of America on acid-free paper

16 17 18 19 20 21   10 9 8 7 6 5 4 3 2 1

First Edition

To my three wonderful sons: Russell, Todd, and Aaron. Thank you for appreciating life and for enabling your mom and dad to sleep with dreams . . . instead of nightmares. The more you are not like us, the more proud we are!

Love, Dad

PS: To my wife, Debbie, *the consummate wife, mother, and grandmother.*

Contents

Acknowledgments

Thanks to Anne Justus, for braving through unending editing and organization.

Thanks to Lisa Harer and Victoria Vega, my coworkers, for allowing me to engage this passion amid a busy day.

Thanks to Nick Lehnert, Tony Madrigal, Rick Mathis, Dan Moore, Bill Noble, Dave Richens, Chris Smith, Bobby Weinberg, and Scott Dickson for keeping me grounded in all things.

Thanks to Roger and Cheryl Spurlock, for modeling terrific grandparenting.

Thanks to Steve Nassau, for brilliant titling and insight to unique thinking.

Entitlemania is not my word. It has been used before in many blogs and parenting articles. Thank you, Laura Kastner, PhD, for encouraging me to use it for the title.

Entitlemania Exposed

"ENTITLEMANIA" APTLY DESCRIBES THE STATE OF MIND IN WHICH children believe they should have anything they want, while also believing they shouldn't have to make any effort to get it. Remarkably, we parents, who are responsible for creating these children, are typically unaware our actions are the single cause of this result.

Whether you are a new parent and are concerned about teaching your young children to appreciate what they receive and to earn what they desire, or if you are the parents of preteens, high schoolers, college students, or adult children, *Entitlemania: How NOT to Spoil Your Kids . . . and What to Do If You Have* will help you recognize what behaviors of yours might be germinating the seeds of entitlement. If your kids are already suffering from this epidemic, as many of our children are, let me show you what you can do to slow this train from barreling down the tracks toward directionless lives, in which your children have yet to make the connection between effort and achievement.

My name is Richard Watts. Some of the richest families in America retain me to shadow their daily lives. As a personal advisor and their legal counsel, my job is to predict obstacles in their lives and figure out how to save their children, and their children's children, from the perils of wealth, which, when applied improperly, can cause kids to become downright train wrecks. Some become unappreciative, entitled ingrates; others seem lost; and still others who start life with every advantage end up drugged out. For thirty years, I have witnessed scores of children grow up and become successful and others become dismal failures. They all have one thing in common: parents.

In my first book, *Fables of Fortune: What Rich People Have That You Don't Want*, we discover the counterintuitive nature of becoming wealthy and examine how the more things we acquire, the more difficult it is to find happiness. My second book, *Entitlemania*, looks at the ways in which well-meaning parents often weaken their children by overindulging them and overmanaging their lives. Moreover, when parents give their children too much, it often prevents those children from recognizing their true aspirations. It takes away their opportunity for discovery and the self-pride and contentment that follows adversity and struggle.

It IS Your Fault

Most well-intentioned parents hope to minimize their own difficulty and maximize their pleasure . . . "I will help you (my child) have a wonderful life, and you will feel good about it . . . and yourself."

Undoubtedly, any parent knows this is easier said than done. All you have to do is look around and you will see children who have been given countless opportunities and guidance at every turn by experienced and loving parents. Yet, despite living in a world of instant access and unlimited knowledge resources, many children appear unequipped for their futures. Why? What did we miss? Our parenting program was thought out carefully and executed with tireless dedication. Our script was a combination of minimizing failure in our kids' lives and providing the opportunities we missed in our own lives either through neglect or lack of money. "We gave our kids everything we ever wanted!"

> **"We gave our kids everything we ever wanted!"**

Does that work? Beware, as Robert Woodson says, "In the process of giving our kids everything we didn't have, we forget to give them what we *did* have."

Convince yourself of this simple and certain truth: *For everything you give your child, you take something away.* Our responsibility as concerned parents is to determine what you are taking away. The self-actualized parents of today exchange concerns over coffee, golf, shopping, and dinners. "When did our children develop this sense of entitlement to what we, their parents, have; what they, the children, want; and what they expect?" These parents experience no cognition of blame and no introspection. "It can't be our fault. Society, college, or peer pressure created these little ingrate children of ours, not us!" Wrong! It *is* us. Feeling entitled isn't a bad thing. In fact, the entitled child doesn't feel entitled at all. It is the parent who feels unappreciated and misunderstood!

Surprise! It's Not New

The entitlement problem, although seemingly a current-day phenomenon, is not a new trend. The nineteenth-century psychiatrist,

Sigmund Freud, addressed it back in his day. This is what he had to say about the process that leads to entitlement:

> "They are impelled to ascribe to the child all manner of perfections which sober observation would not confirm, to gloss over and forget all [their] shortcomings . . . The child shall have things better than [their] parents, [they] shall not be subject to the necessities which they have recognized as dominating life . . . restrictions on [their] own will are not to touch [them]; the laws of nature, like those of society, are to be abrogated in [their] favour; [they are] really to be the center . . . of creation."[1]

Let me make it clear that *Entitlemania* is not a psychology treatise. I have written it to explain how you, as a parent, can minimize the potential damage of your own ideas of good parenting. My conclusions are drawn from the observations in my professional career and personal life. The narratives are based on true stories, although the names of the individuals have been changed to protect their privacy. The stories will provide you with the opportunity to see what has worked and what has failed miserably for other smart parents.

All Is Not Lost

Entitlemania helps new parents anticipate the pitfalls of entitlement, and older parents steer their children back to a life of self-fulfillment and pride. The truth is the process that leads to

---

1   Millon, Theodore. *Disorders of Personality.* Third ed. (Hoboken, NJ: John Wiley & Sons, 2011), page 413.

entitlement can begin even before the child is in the womb. It can continue until the child is in his or her sixties.

Although some of the children described in this book are children of wealthy families, their symptoms are only magnified versions of evidence we see in our own children's everyday habits. Why do our children expect careers to be handed to them? Why do they assume they deserve the same things we worked so hard to earn? How will they learn that life becomes better the harder they climb? Why do parents avoid sending their children to the university of hard knocks, when they themselves struggled and toiled, working to earn postgraduate degrees? When did we conclude that our kids shouldn't have to get too stressed out? When did we start believing our own pride was transferable to our kids?

Let's explore our own world of parenting and seek the truth. We might discover answers to questions we are afraid to ask. Children of entitlement all had at one time parents, a parent, grandparents, or a benefactor who set in motion a course of exposure and training that created a narrow perspective. That perspective created a universe for those children—a universe made up of certain rights, privileges, and assumptions from which the children describe and define their world.

Think of this parental exposure like radiation. It is not very noticeable, or obvious, until a few years pass and your hair starts to fall out.

Think of this parental exposure like radiation. It is not very noticeable, or obvious, until a few years pass and your hair starts to fall out. There is still hope. You can avoid having children who cause you worry during your entire adult life and retirement.

The difficulty in administering the cure, however, will not be in enlisting your kids' cooperation . . . but rather your own.

Let's Get Started

Entitlemania is divided into three sections. The first, *Parents, Check* Your *Attitude*, covers what we, as parents, need to be aware of in our own motivations and desires toward our kids and how those things may interfere with them becoming healthy and happy adults. The second section, *What TO Do*, gives practical advice on positive and intentional things you can do as a parent to help your child grow into a strong, resilient, independent adult. The third section, *What NOT to Do*, helps you better understand the consequences of giving too much, especially when giving feels good and seems to be the right thing at the time. Through the stories I tell, you'll be able to see the likely consequences of such decisions and learn from other's mistakes.

Some stories will make you laugh, because they are similar to your own experience. Others will make you cry, as you recognize, finally, it is time for you to get out of your son or daughter's way and let them become the independent unique individuals they were meant to be. Perhaps when you have finished this book, you will have a better idea of what you may be *intentionally* doing *unintentionally*.

PART I

PARENTS, CHECK *YOUR* ATTITUDE

CHAPTER 1

Trying to Be Best Friends? Big Mistake!

WHEN RUSSELL, THE YOUNGEST OF OUR THREE CHILDREN, reached adulthood, it was obvious his mother was feeling the pangs of the soon-to-be empty nest. She and I treated Russell a bit differently than our two older sons, Aaron and Todd. Entitling and enabling are the politically correct words. Spoiled is more accurate. The older boys were given credit cards for college and instructed vehemently they were to be used only in an emergency. They had each opened a checking account. We gave them a monthly allowance in accordance with a predetermined budget and held them responsible for balancing their expenses within budget.

Russell didn't seem to understand the difference between an emergency and a Starbucks triple-shot Frappuccino. He charged at will. The first couple of months were only a hundred dollars. But then the monthly amounts increased. I was angry at these needless expenditures and a twenty-four percent interest rate that was being charged for a balance that was not paid off monthly. My pet peeve was his purchases at Starbucks. Russell ate breakfast and lunch there and usually had two venti lattes a day. He treated his friends. Fast food was easier than cooking. Russell didn't learn to cook. When I became unscrewed with him on the telephone, his mother would give me an evil look like I was abusing our son. I didn't consider it abuse, since I was thinking homicide. I didn't like being the bad guy any more than she did.

There was one month when I received a credit card bill with the purchase of a cappuccino maker for $500. It was fortunate Russell was three hours away. "What on God's earth were you thinking?" I said. "And who would ever buy a cappuccino maker AT STARBUCKS?"

"Calm down Dad, and listen for a second," he responded. "This was well thought out, and I'm sure you will see the wisdom in my thinking and purchase."

The only reason I didn't respond is because I couldn't speak. My brain was in a nuclear meltdown. "Here's my thinking, Dad," he began. "I sat down and did a spreadsheet on the Starbucks purchases for last quarter. I had an average of two venti lattes a day plus breakfast. I cut out lunches because I discovered my food card for the past two years has included lunches all along, and the salads aren't bad. If you multiply $10 for coffee a day, plus breakfast at $5 a day for the last quarter, it is $1,350 per quarter, which is $4,050 for the school year."

He paused. Not hearing any response from me, he assumed I was beginning to understand his logic. To the contrary, my skull had cracked open and my steaming, liquefied brains were spilling down my shoulders.

"So," he continued, "I bought a cappuccino maker for $500 with an additional per cup cost of $0.42. Considering the same consumption rate, I have saved you and Mom $2,624.46 per school year. And that doesn't consider the cost of the times I treat my friends to coffee, which would now benefit from the reduced rate of the cappuccino maker." He paused for the finale. "As you can see, I've paid for the cappuccino maker in two months!" There were two things that kept me from focusing. The first was the "forty-six cents" on the end of his phrase about how much he was saving us, and the second was his idea that *he* had paid for the cappuccino maker in two months. I was thinking premeditated. It was not a good time to respond.

"I'll call you back," I mumbled.

To which Russell responded, "I'll look forward to it, Dad. Have a great day!"

I didn't allow myself to drive for several hours.

Unfriend Them

It often occurs to me how simple the solution was that first month. Cancel the credit card. So why didn't I? Because I was on a run of successful parenting, and Aaron and Todd had been launched from the nest successfully. Plus, the marital friction that arose when I disciplined Russell was uncomfortable. I later learned the youngest child has a talent. They know how to find the seams. They have watched the older children get disciplined, praised, punished, rewarded, nudged, and slammed. They are like young entrepreneurs. They learn how to maximize the profits and benefits while minimizing the cost. Our struggle with Russell was a progression of smaller events, each probably unidentifiable by itself. We were becoming masters of blind enabling. Our philosophy had shifted from *let's consider each of our children as individuals and carefully apply strictness to what is best for them* to what I call defensive and selfish parenting. We expected Russell to do the following:

1. be as successful as his siblings and

2. bring additional pride to us, confirming our success as parents.

We got lost. The effects of enabling are cumulative. We paid the price later. We should have just canceled the credit card.

After Russell graduated from Pepperdine University, he returned home to our house in Laguna Beach, California. Neither of our older boys was invited to live at home past the first summer after college. Our philosophy was, "Get jobs, and get going!" Each of my older sons secured a job, an apartment, and a George Foreman electric grill, and they set out into the wilderness of life. When I thought back to that time, I realized they did not even ask to stay at home. They understood what the next step was because of the stability and consistency of our parental march.

Russell, however, somehow finagled us into allowing him to base himself at home after the summer while he searched for a career. He wanted stability. He decided to experiment with the commercial real estate business and soon found the beginnings of financial stability. Chasing stability is like chasing a grasshopper though; just as you near it, it jumps away. You never grasp it! Russell's pay rate would increase, and he would buy a newer car. He would get a bonus, and we would discover a new surfboard in the garage. We were thinking, *Three months, and then Russell moves out on his own.* Russell was thinking, *When Mom and Dad pass away, continuing to live here isn't a bad option.*

During Russell's first year at home, our home life changed. In a big way. I had come to love having the house to myself.

No longer. Now it seemed that life at home revolved around providing Russell nonstop, top-flight room service. Dinner was prepared in coordination with *his* schedule. My wife cleaned his room. My sleep was interrupted by late night and early morning arrivals from parties and events. I'm sure alcohol may have been involved. My wife, Debbie, found a renewed mission in continuing her skill in child rearing. Russell was pleased to accommodate.

About two years into Russell's stay with us, we returned from a weekend away to find the house a mess. The fact that Russell didn't think it was a mess was no surprise. Russell had invited a "few" people over. It was more like fifty. My liquor was gone. My collection of fine cigars was gone. Russell later rationalized that the cigars were better off smoked. So I could restock to ensure a fresher quality smoke. When I finally got to my bed and pulled the covers up, hoping to forget the past several hours and get a good night's sleep, my bare feet brushed something very damp, like a wet towel, at the foot of my bed. When I reached down to retrieve it and turned on my bedside lamp, I was holding a wet bikini bottom. No top, just the bottom. Russell was already sound asleep upstairs. My wife and I took off the wet sheets and spent twenty minutes remaking our bed at midnight.

I waited a week. Then Russell and I talked. "What do you think of first when you think of me as your father?" I asked.

"Well, that is easy, Pops," he impatiently replied. "You're my best friend in the whole world," he confirmed with a smile.

"Russell." I spoke quietly. "I want to terminate our friendship and be your father." Russell wasn't even fazed. I'm sure he figured there was a proposal coming rather than an ultimatum.

I continued: "It is my belief that you deserve to find a new best friend who will accompany you into your future and experience the same joys and difficulties life has to offer. And he or she will live a lot longer than me and be there for you when I pass on." Now I had his attention. "My job as a parent is twofold. First, I am here to love you unconditionally. That means I might not like what you do, but I am committed to supporting you emotionally for the remainder of my life so long as you respect yourself, and me. Second, I will provide you with suggestions, only upon your request, on tools that I have learned, and experiences that I have lived, that may or may not help you reflect on your own view of your life."

He was finally listening. "Your mother's and my parenting will not always please you, but you must remember my first commitment: I will love you no matter how things turn out for you. You have my word. My first act as your parent and no longer as your best friend is to give you an original thought." Russell was still attentive and optimistic. "You are going to tell your mother you have decided to move out of our home. You will not now, or ever, tell her we had this discussion. I know you are short on funds. I will pay one-half of your rent for six months. At the end of six months, you are on your own, forever. That means even if you have to push a shopping cart, or sleep in your car, you are on your own. When invited, you may visit our home to share a meal, or spend an occasional afternoon. Otherwise, you will stay away from our house." Russell's face showed a look of fear and rejection.

I felt terrible but was tired of cowering away from what I knew was my responsibility as his parent. We were ruining our precious son. Russell moved out two weeks later. His mom pleaded with him to stay but was convinced this was Russell's desire. My manipulation was justified in my mind only by my love and my conviction that I was doing the right thing. It would have been so much easier if we had started when he was younger.

Lose the Battle to Win the War

Russell has now been on his own for two years. He has more new friends than ever—real friends. He is different. He is unique. He is not like me. We have lunch every couple of weeks and dinner at the house on Sundays. Russell had a tough financial run this past year. We could have helped him. We didn't. He had to vacate his single apartment and find a roommate to share the expense. He could find refuge in our home only for an evening's comfort but had to return to *his* world to continue *his* story. Those two years have not been easy for us. He has asked to spend the night just to hang out. We lovingly said no. Completing a separation only causes lingering pain and suffering unless it's finalized as soon as possible.

A few months later, Russell offered to pay for lunch—an early Christmas gift. While we were sitting across from one another Russell said, "Pops, I haven't shared with you how bad it got financially last year." He looked at me, a little ashamed but still confident.

"Even though I cut back, my expenses got ahead of my ability to pay. I gained a significant amount of credit card debt." He looked down at his lap. "Two of the four cards went to collection, and I've hurt my credit. But I had to make a choice and pay for my apartment, food, and gas. I let my health insurance go. I just had to start saying no to some of the pleasure opportunities and dedicate more than the usual forty hours a week to working to make extra money. I didn't tell you because you had asked me to begin handling life on my own. I did. In the past several months, I have just finished working out deals with each of the credit card companies to put me back on track. It won't be easy, but I realize I have the ability to work through things like this past year and whatever may come in the future."

The voice of temptation to reward him was deafening. He had learned so much. Was it enough? By whose standards? How about helping him just a little with that debt? To lift just a portion of the weight . . . *There I go again, being his best friend,* I thought. How could any loving parent let him continue to suffer when he had made so much prog-

He wasn't suffering.
He was learning.

ress? Answer: He wasn't suffering. He was learning. He was actually enjoying his life more than before. He was directing his own path. He was discovering his likes and dislikes. Making choices. Prioritizing.

So I asked him, "How do you feel about your life now, on your own?"

His answer returned like a fastball directly in the strike zone, "I didn't have a life before, Dad . . . I had *your* life."

I sat back stunned but deserving of his response. (Children rarely avoid the candor that can leave us with a lifetime of brain echo.) He was exactly right. Until we applied appropriate parenting skills, I had allowed the behavior to continue.

"Dad," he said, "I'm wondering why you didn't start helping me with this a lot earlier in my life." The fastball made a crack in the catcher's glove. *You're out!* was all I could think. It was time for Dad to have a seat in the bleachers and accept personal responsibility, along with a touch of humiliation. At the same time, I was so very proud. I felt the kind of pride that comes from sacrificing my own peace of mind to permit Russell to struggle.

Russell has since been completely independent and connects with me a little less, but only because his life is busy with work, friends, and leisure. One memorable night, he asked me to dinner and amazingly pulled out his own credit card to pay—one of those favorite moments in parenting.

"Dad," he said, "I'm sure it took tireless effort and time in raising me. I can't fathom the pain you and Mom must have felt to watch me crash and suffer, yet stand by without helping, and allow me to learn how to find my own way. I'm so proud of myself, and you've also given me a lesson in parenting my own children someday."

There is nothing quite so rewarding as watching your children struggle, find their own answers, and develop their own self-pride as a result.

———

Our personal experience with Russell taught us there is good news: You can repair the setback you may have unwittingly and unintentionally caused to your child (although it is obviously best to prevent it). The bad news? It takes focus and often exhausting perseverance. And when you begin to see results, you must be even more careful, because your desire to intervene and reward will return like a sweet tooth to a chocoholic.

> *You can repair the setback you may have unwittingly and unintentionally caused to your child.*

Be a Parent, Not a Best Friend!

When did we, as parents, decide being our child's best friend is more important than teaching our kids the difficult lessons of life? Why aren't we strong enough to accept that our children may not like everything we teach them? We find ourselves embroiled in the head-scratching exercise of asking, *When did my child gain the notion that life is supposed to be an uninterrupted picnic?*

If you are a parent who has ever said out loud, "My daughter and I are best friends!" or you hear your son or daughter tell people, "My dad is my best pal," perhaps you are failing to deliver to your kids the difficult messages of life. Your child will benefit from you being first and foremost a *parent*. Let them find a best friend their own age.

Sure, it's tempting to become that best friend. And the temptation starts early. Young children are a joy to be around. Their young minds are boundless, imaginative, and uncluttered by emotional history. Being an adult can be exhausting! Sometimes sitting on the floor with a three-year-old assembling a floor puzzle can be as relaxing as a double martini.

As our kids mature, it's fun and personally gratifying to invite ourselves into their world of play and experience being a kid again. It lets you relive the fun you had as a child (and maybe, haven't had since). We are a generation of parents who, by and large, actively participate in our children's leisure pursuits; something people in my parents' generation did not do.

In previous generations, parents were more apt to allow their kids to play and explore on their own. That was certainly true for me. When I was twelve, my best friend Scott and I would ride our bikes from our homes in La Habra Heights, California, to the Whittwood Mall in Whittier, twelve miles round-trip. We would take enough from our piggy banks to go to the theater and buy popcorn, candy, drinks, and ice cream cones with three scoops of Thrifty ice cream for the return home. We'd leave at 7:00 a.m. and try our best to be home before dark. Dinner was at 7:00 p.m., and there was hell to pay for being late. There were no cell phones. Pay phones cost money, and we had none to spare. Being late was not an option.

When we returned at night, our parents were ready fo͏ Sometimes they would ask where we had been, but usually didn't. I don't think they cared. Often, we found ourselves gettin kicked out of movie theaters for throwing popcorn and shooting peas through straws at the other theatergoers. We would ride our bikes into the ground. We had little money, and yet somehow we always figured out how to fix our flat tires. We were rich in experiences. Few parents today are that hands-off. And few permit such unstructured play.

For parents who struggled through hard times and learned from difficult experiences, parenting permits a much-welcomed "life reset" or "do over." What I mean is this: We work doubly hard to make sure our kids don't make the mistakes we did, such as not getting good enough grades in high school to get into a top college, not working hard enough to make the varsity sports team, or spending too much time on hobbies that have no future job payoff. Sure, we have the best of intentions; we want to spare them suffering. But there is another reason. Selfishly, we don't want to suffer through the pain again. It's remarkable, isn't it, how the things in life that hurt you the most are permanently affixed in your brain? It's as if there were a screen just inside your eyeballs from which you can read all your past hurts. It is part of your personal life narrative. Hurts are powerful motivators. They compel you to avoid certain types of events and people for the rest of your life. The desire to avoid pain can cause you to react unconsciously, in a self-protective way, even when you *think* the person you are protecting is your child.

In short, *best friend* parents live vicariously through their kid's pleasures and pain. During the process,

> **Best friend *parents* live vicariously through their kid's pleasures and pain.**

ıte their own kids so they can relive their
r confront and rescript one of their child-

:st friend to a copilot. He sits next to you
ght. You see the same view together. Best
the same level of experience you do and are
present to help you confirm or contrast your thoughts on decisions rendered contemporaneously. They are the same age. When
entering the turbulence of life, one best friend looks to another
(like a copilot) and says, "Looks like we have encountered unexpected winds and unsmooth air." There is comfort in sharing similar experiences. The next action for a youth is to try to improve
the circumstance. "I'm thinking we should change altitude to
thirty-seven thousand feet and look for smoother air," a copilot
might suggest. The decision to go a different course will either
work or suggest rethinking and devising another plan. Again, it's
trial and error, cause and effect. Yes, that experience worked. No,
this one didn't. In that process, pilots gain indispensable knowledge and experience. So do children.

Many parents would rather be copilots with their children
than air traffic controllers. Some par-
ents, unfortunately, try to be both.
Parents should be more like air traffic controllers. They're in the control
tower and see what the pilots don't see.
They track the entire flight; yet, their
role is to respond to pilot inquiry and
advise of irregularities so the aircraft
can avoid catastrophes. Of course, the
air traffic controllers leave the *flying* of
the plane to the pilot.

> **Many parents would rather be copilots with their children than air traffic controllers. Some parents, unfortunately, try to be both.**

The Price of Selfishness

Behaving as if you are your child's best friend can do irreparable damage—to the child, certainly, and in some cases . . . to your marriage as well. This was certainly the case for Brad, his ex-wife Kara, and their daughter, Brianna, who is now an adult and a twice-divorced single mother.

Brad came from money. His grandfather was an original partner in a company that grew to over thirty thousand employees in the twenty-first century. When the stock trickled down to the children and eventually the grandchildren, the family split just under $2 billion. The family also created a name for itself through philanthropy, with its name appearing on the buildings of several prominent universities across America.

Brad and his wife Kara had three children. In addition to Brianna, who is the eldest, they have two sons, Lincoln and Seth. Brad and Brianna, a lean, blue-eyed beauty, were especially close; so close, in fact, that he called her his "Princess" and treated her like royalty.

When Brianna was in grade school, Brad was one of the few dads who played the role of classroom "mom." He coached Brianna's soccer team, took her clothes shopping (even when she was a teenager), and accompanied her when she toured with local beauty pageants.

By age sixteen, Brianna had quite the womanly figure. She loved to wear provocative clothing and swimwear and show off her figure. This didn't bother Brad at all. In fact, he beamed with pride when she paraded on stage, while the moms of the other contestants grimaced over the inappropriateness of her outfits. Nonetheless, Brianna often won. Brad felt like a winner, too.

When Brianna went to her senior prom, Brad insisted on

being a chaperone. At the prom, he danced several times with his daughter so they could show off the dance steps they'd practiced for years. The duo created quite the show.

Brianna was as intelligent as she was beautiful. She graduated with top grades. On her graduation day, she made a fashion statement by wearing four-inch stiletto heels beneath her black baccalaureate gown. After the graduation ceremony, Brianna, still in her cap and gown, walked toward the parking lot with her parents, the other grads, and their families.

Parked in the first space of a completely full parking lot was a bright white BMW M3 topped with a five-foot-tall pink ribbon and bow. Its sunroof was retracted, and a giant pink teddy bear sat smiling in the driver's seat. Written in pink-colored professional lettering across the rear window were the words, "We love you, Graduate!"

The other graduates gathered and gawked around Brianna's *kill*. Her friends acted sincere in their appreciation for Brianna's gift. The other parents showed emotions ranging from pity to contempt. Brad accepted all of it with the genuine smile of a winner.

Brianna's relationship with her mother was more complicated. Brad looked to Kara to discipline Brianna when necessary; in fact, he *always* left the discipline of Brianna up to her. (Brad took on the job of disciplining his sons Lincoln and Seth; he considered it his role as the man to make his sons into strong, self-supporting young men.) Kara sometimes got annoyed at Brianna but said little. What loving mother would criticize a daughter who almost always got it right?

Kara resented having to play bad cop while Brad always played the beloved hero to their daughter. Kara was angry because he was never willing to put his relationship with Brianna at risk, even when setting limits was in Brianna's best interest. The way Kara saw it, it was not always about girls and boys, but more about what was right and wrong. Two years after Brianna graduated from high school, Kara filed for divorce.

Brianna got good grades in college. She didn't fare well with men, however. Many were attracted to her, but she couldn't discriminate between the good ones and bad ones. Although she was popular and well liked, in her intimate relationships, Brianna behaved as if it was all about her. She had known nothing else. How could she? With Brad, it *had* been all about her.

Consequently, the only men who made the effort to pursue her were not interested in her mind. They were users. Others could see this pattern, but Brianna could not. She would commit too easily and then be gravely disappointed. She was sure she had found "the one," and weeks later *she* would break it off. Everyone fell short.

That all changed when Derek proposed to her just after graduation. The destination wedding was planned for St. Kitts in the Caribbean. The guests were encouraged to reserve their hotel rooms well in advance (at the special wedding event rate of $320 per night). It was a four-day extravaganza . . . that never happened. Two weeks before the wedding, after guest rooms could no longer be canceled and wedding gifts had been sent, Brianna and the groom had a fight. She recoiled from his "shallowness and pigheadedness" and retreated to her father, who consoled her by saying, "Derek wouldn't have measured up anyway." Brad thought his princess deserved better. The hotel let Brad off with paying just fifty percent of the expenses ($140,000). The wedding gifts were never returned, and the guests never received an apology for the cancellation. It was never again discussed.

As luck would have it, Brianna found a new prince charming and married him twelve months later. Not so long afterward, she divorced him and remarried a second time twenty months later. This time, she was pregnant. That marriage did not last either.

Brianna is now a single parent raising a little boy, Bradley Jr. And Brad Sr. is the perfect grandfather. He dotes on little BJ. Brad and his new wife set up a trust fund for BJ's education and have included a little extra for the future purchase of his first home. Now Brianna and her mother have a stronger relationship than ever before; they are able to share their loss of trust in men.

So, Whose Fault Is It?

How could this have been avoided? What is worth saving a daughter's life and ensuring she develops into a woman who can have a healthy marriage? Better communication between Brad and Kara would have helped. Brad could have simply asked his wife, "What could I be doing better with Brianna?" Kara might have been more honest with Brad about how much it upset her to play the bad cop. Both could have benefited from professional therapy. Some fathers treat their own daughters like mistresses. The solution? Wife first, daughter second.

Economically, parents should refrain from shocking their kids with unnecessarily extravagant gifts. Modeling modesty is an excellent parental quality. Sacrificial love involves denying yourself control in order to provide lessons only self-experience can teach your children. Would you be willing to live in a neighborhood below your financial means? The concept is right, but our egos rarely allow us to be self-sacrificial for our kids. In the end, which sacrifice costs you more?

> *Sacrificial love involves denying yourself control in order to provide lessons only self-experience can teach your children.*

Can you relate to these stories? Can you see how and why a parent's decision to give, give, give can have such a detrimental effect on the child? Make no mistake—*the parents* are responsible for entitlement in their children. Entitlement is a mini-psychosis instigated by parents, enabled by parents, and acted out by our children.

When we blame our kids for acting entitled, we are deflecting our own responsibility.

CHAPTER 2

Stop Playing . . .
Your Kids Are Not a Hobby

I'VE ALWAYS MARVELED AT THE MIRACULOUS SURVIVABILITY OF a newborn after the horror of being abandoned by its mother, discarded in a dumpster, and not being discovered for a day or more. For me, it has always begged the question—how much more do I need to give my kids that those dumpster kids didn't get? This is terribly crude, but it makes me wonder how much is too much?

The trend these days is just the opposite, especially if you consider how educated, successful young parents—aided and abetted by the Internet—seem to set themselves on a mission to eradicate even the tiniest thing that could make their child's environment less than *perfect*. For these children or "pre-borns," entitlement is already germinating, based on the parents' preconception of child raising, while that child is still in the womb. If the parent carries through with this thinking—that I have to smooth the path for my little one—he or she becomes the stereotypical "helicopter parent." And soon, the child's sense of entitlement becomes hardwired.

The Path to Entitlement Starts Early

Justin and Jenny, married five years ago in their early thirties, exemplify the early stages of this perfectly. They met at USC and are now a modern, two-career couple. Justin is an advanced computer programmer and travels at least three days of each week. Jenny is a chief packaging designer for the creative team of a highly successful cosmetics company selling boutique-quality facial products for teens. They are focused on advancement and helping each other move ahead in their respective careers. And yes, building a family figures into their plans. In fact, they decided to purchase a labradoodle puppy, Baxter, so they could practice parenting.

Predictably, Justin and Jenny approached Baxter's care with the same level of deliberativeness with which they approach their careers. To make sure Baxter had the perfect environment in which to grow, Justin spent an entire Saturday constructing a mail-order doghouse, which would fit perfectly on the patio. When he and his wife heard that a puppy is trainable at sixteen weeks, they signed up and attended obedience school in hopes of owning a well-trained dog. Both Jenny and Justin attended the classes, and each worked with Baxter every day to ensure careful adherence to good trainer practices.

Baxter was obedient, and fun to watch, as he performed several tricks that entertained friends who stopped by to visit. Weekends were consumed with dog parks and trips to dog-friendly destinations where Baxter could remain the center of attention. Of course, Justin and Jenny's social calendar had to be trimmed because they became increasingly unwilling to leave the dog alone for long periods of time, and a pet hotel was out of the question.

When they did travel, they decided Baxter would be more

comfortable if he remained in familiar surroundings and on the same feeding and walking schedule. So they hired Kelly, a local high school girl, to be a live-in caretaker when they traveled.

All in all, the price of Baxter's monthly care eventually cost more than Jenny's dream car, a BMW. After two years of life with Baxter, the three of them began to discuss starting a family (yes, Baxter was included in those discussions).

At the time, Justin, Jenny, and Baxter shared a two-bedroom apartment. Justin's mother, Margie, who came from money, was excited about the prospect of having grandchildren and only too happy to help. She told the couple she'd give them the financial help they'd need to purchase a three-bedroom condo, which she thought minimally adequate space for an expanding family. Justin and Jenny readily took her up on the offer.

Jenny went to the Internet to learn all she could to find the perfect place to raise a child. She diligently researched a host of factors, including proximity to industrial portions of the county; nearness to dust and wind belts, which stirred up particulates; quality of air based on nearness to bodies of water or woodlands; and quality of surrounding hospitals for the initial delivery and follow-up infant care. Ultimately, she and Justin chose the ideal neighborhood and then shopped carefully for the perfect condo.

No doubt, the information available to us from the Internet is astounding and unbounded. Once you become used to sipping from a firehose, you may discover that information overload brings its own brand of anxiety. This is even more true for anxious, new mothers-to-be who want to do everything right. Given the kind of marketing done today, many parents with a conscience feel it's necessary to have their child sleep in an all-organic crib, with eco-friendly wood, nontoxic paint, and an organic mattress made with steel springs and organic foam from a rubber tree. To do otherwise, would put your newborn angel at risk of inhaling lethal chemical vapors during sleep, right? Advertising is focused on getting new parents to believe just that.

Do you see where I am going with this? Expectant moms or dads who train their attention, early on, on even the minutest factors that could harm the baby, are likely to develop into older parents who are in the habit of smoothing every little bump in the road for their growing child. That's why I like to say, *"The path to entitlement can begin with the parents' expectations even before the child is born."*

> **The path to entitlement can begin with the parents' expectations even before the child is born.**

Of course, it's natural to provide intensive care for an infant. But the parent who continues to give at that level of intensity and eliminate every hazard for the preteen, teen, and young adult does so at the very real risk of handicapping that child. The other potential consequence? Making a mess of the parent-child relationship—and perhaps even the grandparent-grandchild relationship—down the line.

Leave the Bumps in the Road

Dennis is the thirty-five-year-old son of Everett and Wendy. Everett and Wendy started and operate a family business that now manufactures seismic fixtures for commercial and high-rise office construction. In recent years, there has not been a sizeable building erected throughout the world that doesn't use one or more of their products. So business has been *very* good. The family owns two yachts in two different bodies of water, and homes in three countries. Each home is staffed year round to allow the family to travel at a moment's notice. Everett and Wendy are generous and well known for their donations to local churches and charities.

When Dennis and his two sisters were young, they had a relatively normal, upper middle-class upbringing. Dennis and his sister went to college. His second sister attended cosmetology school and moved to New York City, hoping to do makeup for the rich and famous. Dennis spent his summer breaks working at an internship in the family business. Most internships offered little or no pay, but Dennis received a normal, but modest, salary for his work. Everett also paid for Dennis's apartment and gas for his car. It was a perk of the job.

Dennis's parents surprised him with a new Audi A6 to take back to school during his third summer working in the family business. They figured he had worked diligently each summer and deserved a little bonus. They paid for the car outright and handed him the certificate of ownership, which showed the car as owned by both Dad and Dennis.

Dennis studied liberal arts and music in school and graduated debt-free with good grades, particularly in music. He played the violin and was quite good. He loved playing all types of music, including country and rock and roll. He was a bit lost when he first arrived home that summer. He found an apartment, a little nicer than the ones he had rented for each of the previous summers. He was used to his independence and preferred an apartment to himself. There was no discussion of the price or who would pay for it. Dad could afford it. Dennis planned to work for the family business until he chose his career path.

The apartment was unfurnished, so Mom and Dennis made a project of furnishing and stocking the apartment with modest but new furnishings. Rachel, Dennis's longtime girlfriend at the time (and now his wife), helped with the selection process. It was understood Dennis and Rachel were going to live together.

After he graduated, Dennis was introduced as a company salesman, but his office was strategically located next door to Dad. The other salesmen did not enter the boss's office unannounced. When neither father nor son had a commitment for lunch, they left together and usually arrived back at the office after a sixty-minute lunch break.

As time passed, Dennis was not as committed to the office as he was during the previous summers. He started showing up late when he had music gigs the night before. These were formal events, such as orchestras for local theater and musical productions. Dennis's reputation as a musician increased, and as it did, so did the time he spent away from the office. Dad was not upset. Dennis was pursuing his dream, and his parents didn't mind financially supporting him. They had the means.

Dennis married Rachel the following year. She was pregnant, and the family couldn't be happier. The wedding was tremendously showy. Dad and Mom were so proud of their son and new daughter. The prospect of being young grandparents gave Everett a new area for achievement. He was entering a new world of grandparenting, and darn it, he would be prepared! In fact, if Dennis wasn't interested in the family business, perhaps the newborn would be! Else Marie was born six months later. Life was good.

A year after Else Marie was born, Everett suggested Dennis consider buying a home. Dennis had no down payment, and his credit was not established enough to permit a mortgage. Dad wanted to create the appearance that Dennis could qualify for a mortgage on his own, so he pulled some strings at the bank and gave Dennis a pay increase to help make the mortgage payments. In time, Dennis moved his family into their new home.

The following year, Dennis approached his father and said he would like to pursue his music career on a full-time basis. The couple also wanted to have another child. A music career didn't pay well. So Everett agreed to pay him the same salary from the company, and allow Dennis to give his passion his full attention. Dennis was in demand almost immediately. The second child, Amy Lynn, arrived a year later.

Everett was very proud. Although his son's home had three bedrooms, Everett thought—and suggested to Dennis—that perhaps a larger home would be more suited to a growing family. Everett lived in a prestigious area of Cincinnati, Ohio— Indian Hill. There were fixer-uppers nearby that would be the right size. Dennis could not afford them, however. So Dennis's parents decided to pay an extra $400,000 down payment on the home so the mortgage would be in line with the current mortgage payment Dennis was accustomed to. Of course, the salary was still drawn from Everett's company, and Dennis maintained an office he had not seen for over two years. He was becoming quite the accomplished musician, and Everett and Wendy couldn't be prouder.

All was well for the next two years. And then a treadmill test detected a heart blockage in Everett's descending aortic artery. The problem was medically corrected, and all seemed well. But Dennis was shaken. The following month, Dennis and Rachel asked to meet with me, their parents' family advisor, to discuss some of their "concerns." Basically, Dennis was worried about his dad's health. Dennis had never considered the consequences of his dad's death. The question was presented unemotionally: "I love my dad and mom. Dad is the only one who can run the company, and if he dies, Mom will have to sell it."

He turned to Rachel as if to get her permission to express BOTH of their concerns. "If the company is sold, I won't have enough money to support my family." He paused and continued, "This predicament is Dad and Mom's fault. But mostly *Everett*."

The use of his father's first name was noticeably cold. "I was just a kid when Everett started paying me too much for a simple college job and, afterward, just stood by and approved as I moved from a single's apartment, to a home, and now an estate."

Rachel nodded in agreement.

"Now we live in a neighborhood with residents twenty years older who know we can't afford to live there without daddy and mommy's help. Our old friends think we are snobs because of where we live. They don't invite us to dinner anymore. My musician friends can't stand me because they struggle financially in the music industry, and they know I don't. So here we are, the perfect family with no friends, completely dependent on the cow's tit to survive, and exhausting ourselves in a music career that doesn't pay enough for us to live in my first summer apartment. My wife and I argue all the time over this. She thinks it's *my* fault!"

Dennis went on, "Rachel and I realize now, although I don't think they had bad intentions, this was a selfish gesture they could have controlled and prevented. It wasn't about *our* lives. It was about theirs. I'm coming to you because I'm completely screwed. I can't start over in business because I have two young children. I can't start over in a career because I'm thirty-three years old. Some kind of structure has got to be put in place to assure my family will not wind up losing everything *we* have built."

Dennis and Rachel were in crisis, but Everett and Wendy didn't have a clue. As far as they knew, they were proud parents with appreciative kids. They had noticed, however, that Rachel was inviting her own parents over to their house more often than she invited them. That's because Rachel felt less turmoil on her side of the family. As a result, Everett and Wendy were given fewer opportunities to visit with the grandchildren. Dennis and

Rachel's apparent favoritism for the maternal grandparents led Everett and Wendy to have serious disagreements about what went wrong in paradise.

Entitlement Begins with Codependence

So what could Everett and Wendy have done differently? Let's step back and discuss a relationship dynamic that is known as *codependence*. Codependence is a term that grew out of the field of addiction counseling.[2] It later came to have a broader meaning. It is now understood to describe any "dysfunctional helping relationship where one person supports or enables another person's addiction, poor mental health, immaturity, irresponsibility, or underachievement."[3] Codependence very much describes the reality of the relationship many current-day parents have with their children.

You ask, why is codependency so bad? Two heads are better than one. Right? Codependency is not what you think. The word is not interchangeable with *interdependent*. Think of it this way: Parent-child codependency is a bit like a heroin dealer who injects his own kid with heroin. Soon the kid is hooked, hopelessly addicted, and looking to find more of the same. Mom and Dad continue to supply them so long as they are retaining control over their kid's life, dictating moves, and manipulating direction. Eventually Mom and Dad get so involved they forget about their own present lives. Who wouldn't seize the opportunity to

---

2   Rosenberg, Ross. "The History of the Term Codependency." From The Human Magnet Syndrome: Why The People We Love Hurt Us. Accessed February 26, 2016. http://humanmagnetsyndrome.com/blog/2013/11/22/ history-term-codependency/.

3   Johnson, R. Skip. "Codependency and Codependent Relationships." Originally posted on BDPFamily.com, July 13, 2014 and found in the article "Codependency" on Wikipedia. Accessed February 26, 2016. https:// en.wikipedia.org/wiki/Codependency.

repeat their own life with the wisdom of hindsight? In the end, calamity occurs, children stumble, and disappointment arrives. The heroin-pusher parent now steps back, looks at their kid, and complains: *"Look at you! You are just a failure. What have you done with your life? We gave you every opportunity!"* In trying to give them everything, you give them less . . . or nothing at all.

In trying to give them everything, you give them less . . . or nothing at all.

Let's look at Everett, Wendy, and Dennis again through the lens of codependence. Everett and Wendy's codependence were evident before Dennis graduated high school. Had his parents known where their choices were leading, they certainly would have made different ones. Here is what they could have chosen and perhaps said, instead:

- *When Dennis needed an internship*: "Dennis, an internship is not available for you at the company. The employees would not treat you as an equal, or as an intern. You are family. They know that. Besides, I'm a terrible boss. If I put our manager in charge of you and pretend he has the power to hire and fire you, he would simply play a game and treat you with kid gloves. You would not learn, or know the reality of a working environment."

- *When Dennis graduated*: "Dennis, I know you could work at the company, and I could pay you a salary to do something I have enjoyed doing, but I'm not sure you would appreciate it. It is really a rather boring product, unless you built the company. For me it is no longer a product but a success story. And unfortunately, this one is mine, not yours. So as a parent, I'm giving you the good news: You are on your own to run your life as you see fit. Go explore the outer reaches of the world, and find something that brings you passion."

- *When Dennis married Rachel*: "Dennis, if you want to pursue music, I would encourage you. Beware: the music industry often makes its artists pay the price of following the passion of an artist, which you certainly are. But your lifestyle will have to match the income you will generate. I'm sure Rachel understands this. She will probably need to work. When you have children, we would be happy to contribute our time and effort to assist. But we will not financially support you. It would not help you. As a parent, I can assure you, if you do it on your own, you and Rachel will have many struggles, but your successes will be sweet, and no one can take those away from you. If your mother and I cage you by supporting a lifestyle you can't afford, you will be less proud of yourself, feel less responsible to Rachel, and eventually you will hate us as parents for making this life easy on you and robbing you of the opportunity to learn the skills to be self-supporting."

- *When Dennis and Rachel needed a bigger home*: "Dennis, we love you enough to let you accomplish life on your own. This may mean you have to stay in the home you have and add on a room or two. But it will be your home, and your mother and I won't be criticized for it being too big or too small. In any event, you will be happier and more satisfied if we just stay out of your financial life. Be assured, as grandparents, we will emotionally bankrupt ourselves giving your children love and encouragement. As parents, we realize that spending our efforts on you, instead of money, will bring your family closer."

Time to Sober Up

As the American cartoonist Walt Kelly has said, "We have met the enemy and he is us." I can attest to that. In my practice, I have surveyed and interviewed a number of rehabilitation centers throughout the country to help my clients provide a soft landing for children who struggle with sobriety. I've had clients whose kids have ventured beyond alcohol and marijuana to the abuse of prescription drugs, heroin, cocaine, and methamphetamines. But treatment extends beyond the user. The parents must seek their own education.

At the world-renowned Hazelton Betty Ford Center in Rancho Mirage, California, which specializes in treatment for alcohol and drugs, the program focuses on the addict *and* the codependent family. Spouses, children, siblings (even aunts and uncles, in some cases) are required to spend a week at the center, attending seminars that aim to teach them how to assist their addictive family member. Family members rarely see the patient in treatment the entire week. The program for the family runs daily, Monday through Saturday from 8:00 a.m. to 9:00 p.m.

Parents spend evenings in Al Anon meetings with other codependent families. Under this program, family members are not permitted to miss even one hour. The reality soon hits them that they are being treated just like the addict in the family. If the family member misses a half day, they don't "coin out," as they say at Betty Ford. They don't "graduate" from the program. What the family program helps family members understand, to a degree, is that they have become as sick as the addicted patient. The parents' drug of choice may not be alcohol or heroin. Rather, they are addicted to managing, fixing, catching, scolding, warning, threatening, and mortgaging their love for the addicted patient.

When a parent becomes codependent in the way just described, two things happen. Let's say we're talking about the father of the addict, for the purpose of this example. First, he loses track of his own life and puts his goals and concerns on hold. To fill that void, the codependent parent "draws down" on the addict and begins micromanaging everything.

Another thing happens: The choices that father makes inhibit the addict from reaching a place where he or she begins to own and understand his or her own illness. The addict begins to rely on the dad to solve her problems and for her dad to pave the way toward her recovery. She accepts his criticism without guilt. She feels ashamed that her dad is disappointed with her. She learns to avoid her shame by medicating herself with her drug of choice. She doesn't see the need to get better. The dad continues to prop her up with his expectations, and eventually they both collapse and fail.

You saw how that played out in the story of Dennis, Wendy, and Everett. In the end, the dynamic only weakened Dennis, created a rift with his parents, and strained his parents' marriage.

The thing to remember at any given point is this: Your child's life is not *your life*. Although it feels counterintuitive to allow self-discovery and mistakes to happen, such actions are crucial to the child's decision process of picking and choosing what life course to take. Before too long, a parent's own desire for perfection for the child turns the parent into an uninvited, meddling interloper, who not only provides play-by-play guidance but often predetermines and enforces the child's course of travel through life.

Trust me, a codependent parent does not even recognize the signs of codependency. They are subtle. It is interesting to remember how many of us grow to middle age before we realize or appreciate that our own parent was overbearing, controlling, and selfish. Do you think your parent acquired that trait in old age? Not likely. A codependent parent was telling you what to do from the beginning. You were brainwashed. You didn't recognize it as a child.

Breaking codependency with your children is about stepping away from your initial reaction or impulse and asking yourself, or perhaps an older experienced parent, *What are the losses to my child if I take control?* It is about becoming a watchful observer and relinquishing control of most decisions. Of course in young children, you have to be mindful of their personal safety, but beyond that, when in doubt, watch, but don't interfere.

When in doubt, watch, but don't interfere.

Be YOU . . . It's Your Life

What can you do if you recognize signs of codependence in your relationship with your child, or children? Breaking the habit of codependency requires you, first and foremost, to recognize that you play a significant role in the problem. Your children don't need a best friend, or worse, a savior to rescue them. Your children need a healthy *you*. They need the independent *you*. The next-door neighbor *you*. The experienced *you*. The *you* who knows them better than they know themselves and who knows how to parent so kids realize the consequences of their actions. You, the parent, are in a better position than anyone else to do this for your kids. Parenting the right way is a little like strapping yourself on a snorting, bucking bronco in a rodeo; who would want to do it? It's a wild and sometimes hurtful ride, but in the end, it's rewarding and surprisingly shorter than you think.

If you find yourself in a codependent relationship with your child, restore yourself to a positive personal direction and purpose. Focus on your own dreams and less on theirs. Take a vacation without the kids. Seek your own happiness, wellness, and contentment first. You will be better equipped to objectively assist in their guidance.

Do you have a serious struggle letting go of doing what you've always done—giving too much, or always smoothing the way for your child? Perhaps you could benefit from professional help. Seek out a therapist who specializes in helping families with codependent relationships. Admit to the professional you are a codependent and you would like advice on how to break codependency, as if your son or daughter were an alcoholic. Substance abuse codependency is not so unlike parenting codependency with your children. If you were raising the kids next door, how would you do it differently from the way you are raising your own? Give it some thought.

> *If you were raising the kids next door, how would you do it differently from the way you are raising your own?*

———

It is natural to want to protect our kids. We all do it. But by doing so, we are also stealing from them. We're stealing the strength and confidence that is forged when they successfully overcome a struggle or challenge. We owe them tough love. We must equip our kids with the tools to handle their life on their own, *before* we exit. Have you ever told your teenage kids you are not going to live forever? That they need experience under their belt because you will not always be here to help them? Try it sometime. It's a good reality check for both you and your children.

CHAPTER 3

Break the Mini-Me Compulsion

ONE OF THE MOST DIFFICULT CONCEPTS TO ACCEPT IN PARENTING is that you don't have title to your kids. Custody, yes; ownership, no. *They are guests in your house, and only temporary guests!*

In fact—and listen up here, you young parents who are whiz kids at work, especially you product designers—the worst thing you can believe as a parent is that parenting is about molding your little possessions of pleasure into adult possessions of pleasure for your own happiness and amusement.

A child is not a product to design, a project to be managed, or a possession to show off. Yet, if you look around you, you'll see plenty of people treating their kids as if they are possessions in the way their cars and houses are. And you'll see others who seem to think that because they can command their assets, they'll be able to manipulate their kids into doing their bidding. Some succeed; others have kids who flat-out refuse. Either way, it damages the relationship.

Whose Life Is It Anyway?

One of the most selfish things parents can do is parent through the lens of their own narcissism. This is a hard one to see, because most parents who have this flaw fail to recognize it in themselves. However, it's often blatantly obvious to others. One way to check yourself when you have an expectation of your child—ask yourself, *Is this my child's expectation or mine?* If you are the parent of a child who plays sports and you find yourself pacing the sideline and/or barking comments rather than cheering the child on, you are exploding with expectations. You are most likely an embarrassment to your child, your spouse, and perhaps the whole community of supportive parents. If when your child completes a task your first response is, "You could have done better!" then your expectations are damning. As parents, we have our *own* lives, complete with successes and failures. Your child needs to develop *theirs.* The only one preventing them that freedom is you. Take a seat. You can think better with your mouth closed.

For some parents, these expectations extend far beyond the child's performance in school and in athletics. They see the child as an extension of themselves, as someone whose purpose is to fulfill what they could not.

This was the case with Katya, a Ukrainian immigrant married to Andre, a thoracic surgeon in Yorba Linda, California. Tara was their daughter. Katya was very strict with her. She insisted Tara succeed academically. There were not many children in elementary school with a private tutor at the home three nights per week, especially for somebody like Tara who was already the brightest girl in her class. It wasn't enough for Tara to do well in school; Katya also decided Tara should try her hand at tennis. Mom was not interested in Tara just being good at the sport; she wanted excellence. She expected her daughter to be the best.

Boris, a famous retired tennis pro, was retained to begin this process. Lessons were unrelenting and occurred as often as Tara's schedule would allow it. Cost was no object.

Katya had played tennis in Russia and was a rising star. Her family, however, was poor and couldn't support her. She had been on her own. When she arrived at the national level, her natural talent was not good enough to take her where she always dreamed she'd be. She fell short of her dreams to compete at the international level.

Her daughter, however, won almost every match, even before she had professional coaching. She dispatched kids older than her. This came easy to Tara. When her new coach saw her play, he, too, banked on this opportunity to create a prize client who would bring him great recognition. Katya would not let anything distract Tara from her tennis and her studies. It was the perfect combination to land her a scholarship to a major university.

When Tara turned sixteen years old and suggested getting a car to drive, Mom gave her the two-year-old family Range Rover and bought herself a new car. When Tara wanted clothes, or wished to travel with her friends, it only took a request. Tara mentioned that perhaps it would be fun to play volleyball. Mom was dismissive of her request. Mom saw no future in that sport or any sport other than tennis. Tara soon learned not to ask for things she knew her mother would not approve of.

Tara's work ethic at tennis was not strong. That angered both Coach Boris and Katya. The routine was mapped by Boris and implemented by Katya. Tara was only a passenger on the train of her own life.

In Tara's junior year of high school, she was required to take an art class as part of her curriculum.

> *Tara was only a passenger on the train of her own life.*

She tried oil painting. She wasn't great, but she loved the way she could express her emotions with the subject and the colors. She wanted to get better. Her art teacher encouraged her, and over a few months she noticed the improvement. One day, Tara decided to take her artwork home to work on in the evening. When Mom saw this, she clapped her hands fiercely together and snapped, "You don't have time for distractions!" Mom grabbed the unfinished art from the easel and carried it out of the room. To Tara, this felt like punishment. It was the first talent Tara really had to work at. She felt her own motivation had improved her skills. She was proud. Then she felt frustration. Soon she was mad.

This is when the recalcitrant teenager began a war with her parents, particularly with her mother. They stayed mainly at odds until Tara's tennis scholarship and first year at Stanford University took her away to school. It wasn't long before Tara was ranked number three in the country at university tennis. Her studies became secondary. Her life became a work camp. She was a slave to the tennis racquet. Professional tennis, the glamour, the money, and the fame were all in sight. But for who?

Tara resented the pressure, so she hesitated to connect with her mother. When Katya called, Tara would usually put the phone down on the sofa and walk away for several minutes. Then she would pick up the phone to find her mother still talking and say, "Mom, I have to go to class." Katya would immediately recognize the priority and end the conversation. Tara wasn't really going to class.

Tara had declared her major at the beginning of the year. She chose art history. It was now midterms, and it seemed surreal that Katya, the expert at hovering over her daughter, had no idea what Tara was studying in school. But Mom was a laser when it came to Tara's tennis, memorizing the entire season's tennis schedule and researching each opponent as the match neared.

Tara occasionally traveled internationally for her tennis matches. An art museum was always nearby! She was more excited about visiting the Louvre or the Uffizi than she was about improving her ranking and winning a match against the number two seed tennis player in the world. She could sit an hour in front of a famous painting, like Renoir's *Sunset at Sea*, often in her tennis uniform, and imagine the scene acted out in her mind. Sometimes her emotions were so strong about the art, she would cry.

She was a walking paradox: her love of art history, her pain of commitment, her lost dream of a mother, and her future without any personally driven vision. Tara had given up her opportunity to dream about art or any other interest she might have enjoyed. She didn't believe she had the freedom to live her life the way she wanted.

Understanding arrived while Tara was sitting at the Louvre staring at the *Mona Lisa*. She knew that face. But the lady in the painting had been dead for centuries. She knew what others wanted her to be. Yet Leonardo da Vinci exposed her. She was not happy. She was not sad. She was *empty*. The museum guard posted near the *Mona Lisa* thought Tara was sobbing because of the beauty of the masterpiece, but Tara was crying because she felt dead inside. The art she loved so dearly had finally made the lesson clear. It had taken years, but the art held her calmly, patiently, and provided the compass that was missing. Then, just as the Olympic Trials were beginning with a guaranteed place for Tara on the Olympic team, at a moment when her proud coach and even prouder parents were about to introduce a female sports rocket to the cosmos, Tara quit the sport.

Once Tara announced her decision, her mother was crushed. Dad was supportive and a little oblivious to all the fuss. The university allowed her to finish her degree in art history without pulling her scholarship. Tara's life outside of tennis was both frightening and exhilarating. It was all a discovery, and she was an infant in so many areas of experience. She and her mother broke off contact for nearly two years. Katya was angry. Mom's life had been ruined, again!

Dad called Tara periodically and was supportive. Tara would always remember one comment her dad made after the debacle: "If you love art the way I love medicine, enough to give your life to it, then I know you will be happy." Tara was happy.

And after Katya had her fill of silence, she once again connected with Tara. After agreeing never to discuss Tara's art career during future calls, their relationship limped to repair. Mom never apologized. After all, she believed that what she had done had been for Tara's own good.

Fortunately, Tara had the strength to find her way to the life she was meant to live, and she put aside the one that would have made her a prisoner of her mother's unlived dreams. Tara liked struggling as an artist. Art made her feel alive, and it continued to challenge her. It satisfied a need only Tara could recognize. A small amount of honest praise for her improvement was worth a hundred tennis match victories.

She had found her passion, and she was happy. Isn't that what every mom and dad wants for their child?

How selfish of Katya to think that her own expectations of her daughter were the ones that mattered. In her selfishness, she nearly destroyed her relationship with her daughter.

As Katya learned the hard way, raising children is often like the primary rule in riding a bull. The more rigid you are, the more likely you are to be ejected.

Conversely, the more relaxed and patient you are, the more you will sense the torquing and twisting as it occurs. And sometimes, when neither works, you just hang on and accept a few bruises and an occasional broken spirit. If you survive, the bull will respect you. It knows. And if you get bucked off, you dust yourself off, get back on, and try again. Understand: It is not about breaking the bull. Unlikely. Not all kids are bulls, but every good kid is part bull. Let them make noise. Then help them turn their noise into the music *they* want to hear.

Whose Dream Is It?

Not all parents go overboard the way Katya did, but if we're being honest, we all have to allow that some of our reasons for wanting to be good parents *are* selfish. Raising "good" children is part of the criteria we use to grade ourselves. If we're successful, we increase our emotional net worth. Our efforts can be more about us than the child, more about our dream than the child's dream.

How can you curb this?

First, learn to discriminate between your expectations for your child and their desires for themselves. Then take the focus off of *your* expectations. Discover theirs.

Second, realize that self-discovery—and the freedom to make mistakes—is crucial to a child's development. Don't forget—it was the school of hard knocks that carved you into who you are today.

Third, when in doubt, watch but don't interfere. Relinquish control, and let your children find their own way.

Fourth, realize that maturity is about having the freedom to choose, as opposed to having others choose for you. If you want your kids to mature, you have to give them the appropriate level of freedom to choose for themselves.

Fifth, and most importantly, help your child identify his or her uniqueness. All children have some quality that makes them unique, in a good way. Look closely to see where your child has a special trait, passion, interest, or voice that's different from the herd. Then appreciate that originality in them and encourage them to develop it. If that gift isn't something the rest of the world appreciates, make sure to explain that their second-rate skills in soccer or below-average grades are only small pieces of the whole cloth that makes them uniquely who they are.

Finally, realize that it takes personal maturity and exhaustive creativity to find a way to encourage our children to be the best they can be.

The Prisoner WILL Escape

Kelly Millet was born into a family of privilege in Greenwich, New York. She and her brother and sister were raised in a home large enough for five families, a home with a lawn that took almost an entire day for a team of gardeners to mow.

The Millets were a Wall Street family. Dad was a senior-level investment banker for Goldman Sachs. His income, even in the 1980s, was millions of dollars a year. Mom was a beautiful stay-at-home mom who was involved in every community organization in town that mattered. She was a little obsessed with painting a picture of the perfect family. She was concerned when her son was born with ears that flipped out a little at the top, but she knew that could be fixed with cosmetic surgery when he reached his teenage years.

Nothing was spared in raising their family. The kids attended a private school. Mom had signed a waiting list six years earlier, when the first child was born. The $5,000 per year donation to hold the spot was little compared to the tuition in 1990 of $18,000 a year . . . for kindergarten.

Of course, the Millets had the privilege of one of the school's ten "reserved" parking spaces, which Mr. Millet acquired by putting down the winning bid of $15,000 at the annual charity auction each year to raise money for the school's athletic program. That amount bought one parking space for one year, but it also bought the family status. Mr. Millet would have happily paid $25,000. (Shh!)

Kelly was a brilliant student but had a wild side. Her older sister was more like her mother. Together, the girls consumed most of the awards and accolades at the National Assistance League. To the Millets, it was always about appearances. Kelly received a lot of attention. She had the type of beauty that was hard to look at directly. Her eyes were as blue as the ocean. *She must be perfect*, thought everyone in town. But on the inside, Kelly was imploding. Every time she even slightly disappointed her mother, she felt guilt. But no one was looking inside. Kelly knew her appearance of being perfect was all that counted to her mom.

When she was fourteen, she turned to the family liquor cabinet for comfort. If she wasn't allowed to make her own noise, she would douse the flames of individuality with vodka. She continued to drink throughout high school, and when she graduated from high school, she turned to cocaine instead. She could afford it.

No one seemed to notice. But her family did notice the several beautiful tattoos she got during her teenage years. *That* did shame them.

Despite her cocaine addiction, Kelly went to college. Two years into college, Kelly met a graduate student, William, who was interning at Goldman Sachs, making him the perfect catch for a husband. Within a couple of months of dating, she was pregnant. Her family was horrified. It was not possible. What would the folks back home think?

Kelly and William married. Kelly completed her education,

and after a brief stint working for a Wall Street firm, she quit and became a full-time mother. She was convinced she could make her new family life more authentic than her own. But William was traditional and had been raised in a family very similar to Kelly's. As a result, Kelly soon felt that she was being placed in the same box as her mother.

Kelly became pregnant again, and she seemed to be handling the pressure. However, after the baby was born, she turned back to vodka. And her nights belonged to sleeping pills.

For three years, Kelly endured the whining of her mother, sister, and sometimes her younger brother. They warned her of the path she was on. But Kelly was not on a path. She was off-road.

After three vacations in a world-class rehab center and two relapses, she took her two children, left New York, and divorced William. She was running. William should have taken the kids, but his career took precedence. Kelly landed in California and found a job at a mid-level rehab center. She was hired to be the representative who would introduce families of future patients to the unique features of the facility and its programs.

Her mother called all the time, trying to control Kelly through guilt. Her mother thought it would be helpful to keep reminding Kelly that she had ruined her life and that her kids would unfortunately repeat the tragedy when they grew up, because she was such a poor example. Mom's behavior was destructive and demeaning and only added to Kelly's poor image of herself.

Kelly decided contact with her mother was too painful. The next time her mother called, Kelly explained she would only take her calls once a week, and if Mom said anything negative or discouraging, Kelly would hang up. That made things better.

Somehow, Kelly had known since her youth that Mom and Dad's path in life was not right for her. At first, she thought she could take herself off the path. But when that didn't work, she had done the only thing she knew to destroy the life she didn't want anyway.

But after she set some boundaries around the phone calls, she sensed the slate was now clean. There were no reminders she was failing at someone else's life. She wanted her own. With a four-year-old and a two-year-old, holed up in a one-bedroom apartment, she finally felt she owned her own destiny. It didn't matter that it wasn't glamorous. It was hers. That was enough.

Several months later, difficult financial circumstances grew worse. She became pregnant, again. She gave birth to her third child. Having the child empowered her. The challenge was *her* challenge. She embraced it. She felt her inner strength.

But what of her future? She continually turned down her family's offers of financial support. It was important to Kelly to brave this journey alone. It was molding her. She could feel the improvement. There were no pony rides for her kid's birthdays, no clowns, and no crowd of thirsty kids waiting to be entertained. They sat in the park with a couple of friends they had met in the apartments. It was real. And Kelly liked to practice being real. It was fresh.

Kelly found great passion in helping others with addiction problems. She understood them on so many different levels. It was then that she began to see her own reflection for the first time. No longer did she look in the mirror and see an imperfect version of her mom. She saw reality. Her life stabilized, and with what others considered a ship's hull laden with barnacles, she was gliding through the water of experience. When she met people for the first time, she would confess, "I'm a tattooed drug addict who is just taking it one day at a time!"

Yikes! How do you respond to that? You respond with honesty. That was Kelly's gift. Honesty was no longer a threat. It was a human grenade to other's barriers. She was a Trojan horse.

Within minutes, people who met her saw the real Kelly. And a few minutes later, they were fully revealing themselves. People benefited from meeting her. She helped them see who they really were.

The story could be left there. It's good enough. But the breeze of life is always blowing. Both opportunity and setbacks are never far off. If kids are allowed to become educated about their own nature, and recognize the difference on their own, they will choose the opportunities that best suit *them* and have the character to survive the setbacks that don't. At some point after Kelly had made her break, her sister called her and asked her advice. She was not happy in her life. She needed direction. The next year her mom called. Hanging up the phone, Kelly cried after her mother admitted Kelly was living life with the sense of freedom she had always dreamed of. Her mother said Kelly was the rock in their family. She was the explorer. She was the frontiersman. And the wilderness had become her friend.

> *If kids are allowed to become educated about their own nature, and recognize the difference on their own, they will choose the opportunities that best suit them and have the character to survive the setbacks that don't.*

After several Christmas holidays back home visiting her parents, even Kelly's hometown was secretly impressed with the real Kelly. Many were jealous. They found comfort in the excuse of thinking it was something about California, a liberal population of drugs, sunshine, Hollywood, and generally irresponsible people that had helped her craziness.

The icing on the cake was William. He realized what he had

loved about Kelly all along was her unwillingness to settle. She was stronger than him, and he admired that. William relocated to California and, after dating his former wife for a year, moved in with her three kids and a girl who insisted the road to perfection didn't have enough curves. After being together for two years, they remarried and now have a fourth child!

Moral of the story: Kelly's parents gave her a lot of material things she didn't really need but very little of the love and nurturance she truly needed. When appearances are what matter most, and children are made to conform to support an image, rather than loved as they are and allowed to be the unique individuals they were born to be, the fallout can be disastrous. Some individuals like Kelly are resilient enough to heal and rebuild, but many aren't.

SUFFERING IS A GIFT

Parents of mentally or physically disabled children have to deal very early on with the realization that their child is not the kind of child they envisioned raising. For instance, the announcement your child has Down syndrome *brings on a sense of horror and sorrow. Parents mentally dive off the cliff created by their own expectations, realizing they will never have a "normal" child. They will never be able to lead the kind of normal life they expect. Their child will never play with other "normal" children, nor grow up to have a "normal" family and children of their own.*

I imagine that in the beginning these parents have private thoughts such as, I had such high hopes, dreams, and expectations for my own happiness with this child, and there is no way this child is going to fulfill my dreams, requirements, and demands.

Yet, some are able to get past this. They rebound, rethink, retool, rearrange their priorities, and begin the process of learning how to raise a unique child. The incredible result is most of these families, in readapting their own future to a different life, experience a whole new perspective on their own expectations and begin to accept whatever level of experience their special child will experience. And in the process of learning how to manage that child, these parents learn to manage their own expectations.

Ultimately, they begin to experience the joy and success of that child and gain a completely new appreciation for life's small things. Ask one of these family survivors what their experience has been. Most will tell you it has been exceptionally hard and amazingly rewarding.

Who Defines the "Perfect Life"?

For some parents, the issue isn't that they're trying to live their unfulfilled dreams through their child. The problem is they can't seem to accept any character traits or perspectives outside the narrow bounds of what they've come to see as "normal," or "good." In short, they insist on conformity.

It is frustrating to see parents harness a spirited child this way, and later, if that child has been strong enough to stay true to himself, for those parents to credit themselves with his, or her, success. This is repeated in my line of work, often.

Let me tell you about one young man I truly admire. I'll call him "Kyle." This young man is definitely his own person.

Like his siblings, he showed an early talent for athletics. In high school, he played basketball and football and made the

county all-star teams in both. He was recognized as one of the
all-star high school athletes.

He also earned good grades in school. So far, he sounds like
the kind of son any parent would be proud to have, right?

Well, Kyle was also defiant and mouthy. He made his father
furious.

I remember one particular visit to the family. As I was walking in through the front door, I saw an eleven-year-old Kyle
flying through the air from the kitchen to the family room at
an altitude of over seven feet. I couldn't see his dad, who was
apparently the one who had launched that flight. Fortunately,
Kyle missed the big screen TV and landed headfirst on the family room sofa.

"Did anyone file a flight plan for that aircraft?" I asked as I
entered the kitchen.

I could see his dad was red in the face and perturbed again
with whatever Kyle had most recently done. We often discussed
how difficult Kyle was, why he needed constant disciplining, and
how disappointed his dad felt about Kyle's disrespectful behavior. He was the "problem child" in their otherwise idyllic family. What was their family to do? Kyle, then age eleven, was too
young to send to the army.

Nonetheless, what I saw in Kyle was a very intelligent, discriminating youth, formulating his own criteria for evaluating
the world. He might have been tough to raise, but so is a wild
horse. And think of how beautiful a wild horse can be, even if he
won't take a saddle.

To the family's consternation, Kyle proved just as difficult for
his teachers. In junior high school, he did not hesitate to tell his
teachers exactly what he thought of their effectiveness as teachers. It didn't matter that he was a preadolescent and they were

adults or that he was calling out the teacher in front of the other students. If he didn't think the teacher was teaching effectively, or the instructor hadn't done enough work to prepare for the class, Kyle didn't hesitate to offer his unsolicited opinion. He was brutal in his candor.

More often than not, his perceptions were on target. But that didn't score him points with anyone. His parents wanted him to put up and shut up, to do everything the teachers said, get good grades, and keep a low profile. The teachers complained about his "disrespect," and the principal suspended him several times for his candor in class. At one point, he was put on disciplinary probation and came close to being expelled from the school.

Obviously, his parents were furious. They couldn't understand why Kyle couldn't learn to keep his opinions to himself. But Kyle wasn't built that way. He was unwilling to pretend he didn't see what was clearly in front of him and would not let the truth be muzzled. It was almost his compulsion. He called a lot of people out—teachers, administrators, his parents, and his friends—when he thought it was warranted. He's the kind of person who can see the truth. Most people can't handle the truth.

He was also the kind of kid who could not be bullied. It didn't matter how much larger the other kid was. Kyle stood his ground, and he had power that belied his size. His peers learned not to mess with him.

As Kyle matured into a teenager, he shot up to 6' 7", filled out, and became immense. On the football field, he was able to run forty yards in 4.4 seconds. He became such a standout in basketball and football that Stanford University offered him a full ride for all four years.

Even there, Kyle was his own person. He earned his bachelor's degree and pursued his masters. Counselors at Stanford advised him against this while playing on the football team, but he did it anyway. In fact, he graduated with two masters degrees. You gotta love a kid with that much spirit.

After Stanford, Kyle played for a time in the NFL, but his career was cut short fairly soon because of injuries he sustained. From what I can see, however, his life is just beginning. He is led only by his own passion and the conviction that he can accomplish anything he desires. I don't think Dad could, or would, want to pitch him across the room into the couch again! It wasn't the life course Dad or Mom would have followed, but what a story! How proud they are now!

With a child like Kyle, a parent's patience is tested. Yet you have to provide such children with an extreme amount of patience. Be as tolerant as you can and let him or her experience the consequences or push back of their actions. How others respond to them will either cause them to curtail the behavior or strengthen their convictions. As for me, I'll choose the bronco over the lamb any day!

———

With the best of intentions, we often get in the way of the story our children want to write. So if your daughter wants to be a beautician instead of attending a liberal arts college, what is so wrong with that? Why shouldn't that be recognized as being as much of an accomplishment as your son who attended Stanford University on a football scholarship? The world is made up of doctors, lawyers, vacuum salespeople, store clerks, mechanics, and tattoo artists. Would you love any one of them less if they were yours?

Parenting is something very special, and if performed correctly, it's an arduous discipline that involves learning to maintain a love and vision while recognizing that *reaching the summit is not as important as the climb.* Parents shouldn't care what mountain their child is ascending; just that they learn to climb, fall, recover, and climb again. Consider how presumptuous it is for parents to select the mountain for their child to climb and then badger them constantly to climb the mountain *their* way.

Some kids, like Kyle, have enough inner strength to survive that kind of pressure. But plenty of kids don't.

PAY ATTENTION TO BIRTH ORDER

How does birth order relate to the entitlement process? Here is what I have noticed. The first-born child is often the most dynamic. He or she seems to have more edge. If only one of your children gets arrested, goes to jail, gets divorced, or even fails at anything, it is typically the oldest child. Why? Consider your level of experience as a parent when you had your first child.

Like Chuck Yeager, the original test pilot for the X-15 (the first supersonic rocket launched in our history), we new parents strap in and apply what little knowledge we have to a completely foreign situation in a craft with controls we have never tested, with fervent hope we don't crash and burn. Sometimes we do.

Much of the instruction results in oversteering. For some reason, parents of the firstborn want to force-feed their own childhood experiences. It's as if the parent has a sense of being in a race to have their child reach maturity. If the child can handle thirty miles per hour, then it's time to go forty miles per hour. If they can handle the highway, then it's time for a freeway. But all of this assumes a straight line in raising children. And that never happens.

Along comes the second child. She watches the raising of number one. She has received second-hand training from each success and punishment of her older sibling. She also learns to sneak around obstacles to accomplish her desires. If number one fell in a crevasse of life, causing a huge panic in the family, followed by conflict, upset, and restriction, then obviously number two just walks around it. It doesn't take a genius to avoid the opportunity to sneak a permanent tattoo, over getting good grades and receiving a pat on the back from Mom and Dad and maybe a new car as a result!

Typically, if child number one was successful, Mom and Dad apply the same playbook to child number two and expect the same results. This is not wise. A good gamble, but it is fraught with mistakes. Child number two requires the same attention. Maybe more. Every child is a new mountain to climb, each distinct and unique.

Parents need to caution against being tired and a little lazy. Rather than insist number two follow the path, intentional parents need to encourage the second child to walk off the manicured path created by raising number one. This is not to suggest heroin use, or rampant sexual behavior, but merely that they carve their own path. The second child will respect and appreciate your sacrifice. If number one became the deputy district attorney, number two may make a great chef. The firstborn may criticize the second child because she "got it easy." Yet, the firstborn will also intuitively realize he got something very special. If number one doesn't deplete his energy attempting to parent number two, he will most likely have good future skills in parenting his own children.

Assuming families continue to have children, at some point the "baby" is born. By then parents are already on autopilot. They are tired and don't want unrest, or a crying baby, in the home. The baby knows exactly how to let the parents and the family have peace: "Just give me what I want." One might think the skill level of the last-born is keen from so much experience observing what has gone before. Unlikely. The baby is most likely the happiest in a pure emotional sense, but the least dynamic. These children are experts at "going along" until they want something different. Once they get what they want, they go along some more. Also, Mom and Dad begin to feel they were tougher on the older siblings, and therefore owe the baby something. This equals penance for Mom and Dad, so they spoil the baby. It's hard to fault parents at this stage of life, but candor is more valuable. The same effort made with the first child should be made with the last child too. They deserve it. You owe them.

PART II

WHAT
TO DO

CHAPTER 4

DO Delay Gratification

WHY DO OUR YOUNG PEOPLE EXPECT INSTANT RESULTS AND immediate gratification? Why do they get frustrated so easily? It seems to me they're looking for life's elevator, and they don't want to take the stairs. Sure, technology is speeding things up, and access to information is instantaneous. So even when they're doing research, they're not used to waiting long to get the results.

If you think technology is entirely at fault, however, let me ask you a question. When your child wants, or *demands*, a nonnecessity, how quickly do you give in, if at all? Are you the parent who always says yes? Or are you the one who is chronically annoyed at the other parent for always saying yes?

In many families, this call-and-response pattern—child demands and parent quickly satisfies the demand—starts very early. Children can start to become spoiled as early as two or three years old, which is when they are first able to process signals from the parent and surroundings. Give in to a demand immediately, and the child begins to expect that as the normal course of events.

The pattern you set up with your child has everything to do with what you experienced as a child, although your response to your upbringing is not predictable. Did you work hard for everything you received? Or did everything come easily? How did the events of your childhood forge your outlook on life? What are *your* wounds? What bugged you most about the environment in which you were raised?

Were you the less-talented sibling growing up? Did older sister get treated better than you? Was older brother the better sportsman? Who got most of the accolades from Mom and Dad? Did you grow up having to earn everything? Did you feel jealous of those around you who seemed to get everything so easily? And how does that shape how you respond to your own children?

Overcoming Your Own Childhood

In the case of my wife Debbie, the wounding came from her interactions with an abusive father and stepfather, which caused the drama in the family. It was hell at her home much of the time. Police were called to their home periodically in the middle of the night to quell domestic disputes. When Debbie was eight, she felt the stares of her neighbors on their front porches in her cul-de-sac at 2 a.m., as the bright twirling red and blue lights of the police cars lit up the entire block, and police officers took her father away in handcuffs. Those other families appeared to be so normal and happy.

When she was fourteen, she wanted to try out for the cheerleading squad, but she couldn't because she had to flip burgers at a local department store café to help pay the expenses of her single mom. When she was sixteen, and the transmission fell out of her used car, she got her first loan to pay for the car repair. Because the loan took two weeks to complete, she either rode her bicycle to school or walked until the loan was finalized and the car repaired.

She knows the value of struggle, and she does not help our kids take shortcuts. Yet when she sees me become too firm with the children, she experiences her dad's dominance and feels the pain all over again. So she takes the kid's side and tells me to lighten up.

In some cases, negative personal history can cause parents to be overforgiving and give in to the whims of their young children. In other cases, a similar childhood endows the parent with the fortitude to let baby cry until he finds the quiet of sleep. Debbie experienced that in her own childhood many times.

The behavioral fork in the road begins early. You can choose the easier path and placate your children now, but pay the price later. Or you can choose the bumpier road now and use every opportunity that presents itself to teach your kids that taking the shortcut now will cause their life to be rougher as they mature. In essence, taking the easy road now is a detour from essential life lessons. The longer you stay on it, the longer it will take and the more difficult it will be to get back on track. If you defer these lessons until they are teenagers, you might find a lot of mountainous terrain needs to be covered in returning to normal.

The process of teaching a child to tolerate frustration and delay gratification of a desire, either until the appropriate time, or until the child has earned the desired object, takes constant effort. I won't lie; it is tiring. Giving in to your kids early in life starts the trickle that can become a roaring waterfall as they reach teenage years. Know that laziness around this battle when your kids are young will eventually cause you great frustration. As time goes on, when you have less energy, you will find it harder and harder to deny your children what they want each time they face a struggle or disappointment. It will become *your* fix instead of theirs.

The Motivation Killer

One consequence of giving your children everything they want, instead of teaching them to work for what they want, is it dulls their motivation. Says American psychologist, Dr. C. George Boeree: "If you don't have enough of something—i.e., you have a deficit—you feel the need. But if you get all you need, you feel nothing at all! In other words, they cease to be motivating."[4]

A darker problem is that immediate gratification can ultimately open the door to problems with later substance abuse.

A local high school teacher, Keith, was recently asked why he thought the drug problem among students was so prevalent, even when most were from moderately successful families. His answer? "Immediate gratification!"

When asked to explain how drug use can be tied to immediate gratification, he responded, "Easy! Today's kids are looking for constant activity and fun. They are not used to struggling. Mom and Dad usually help out with that. Instead of working hard to get good at something, they just move to another new activity. Somewhere along the way a friend suggests trying a drug. Whether it's marijuana or cocaine, it doesn't matter. It makes them feel good instantly! There is no effort. When they want to feel good again, taking drugs is a lot easier and more pleasurable than learning to play tennis or golf. Soon, the drug may have them addicted, and before too long the well-intentioned student

---

4   Boeree, C. George. "Abraham Maslow, 1908–1970. Personality Theories." Accessed February 26, 2016, http://webspace.ship.edu/cgboer/maslow.html.

is fully involved in increasing doses and frequency of drug use to get an instant state of well-being. No struggle, just fun. Eventually, they lack motivation to put the time into anything that takes effort to achieve. The root," he suggested, "was getting too much too quickly, too early."

Perhaps the best way to help your children say no to drugs is for you to say no to giving them everything and fixing everything in their lives.

Learn to Appreciate the Journey

So how can you help your child learn they don't get to have everything they want, the minute they want it? I've already talked about the need to say no, and when appropriate, to explain the reasons why you are saying no. The best thing you can do, by far, is model the behavior yourself.

Self-discipline must start with you. How do you measure up? Do you have credit card debt? Do you have a car payment? Credit cards and installment debt are also designed around immediate gratification. Why wait for something when you can have it now and pay for a little piece of it monthly over the next five years? How would you expect your children to learn restraint from someone who is not restrained themselves?

The most helpful tool available in keeping your sanity in the presence of so many "things" is to *exercise not having*. That's right. Here is an exercise. Select something you really want. Something you *can* afford to purchase, or make payments on ... *and then don't let yourself have it!* Instead of trying to ignore your desire to have that thing, talk about it often. "I really want to buy a new set of golf clubs with alloy stabilizing technology, but I'm NOT going to allow myself to have them!" People will think you're nuts! Tell your kids. Tell your friends. But don't give in. You will find most of the time you either didn't want it that badly, or you didn't need it after all, and the result is being satisfied with what you have. Or, when you buy the clubs a year later, you will have a burning desire to have them. And they will be a newer, better model of the clubs you almost purchased. This is excellent modeling.

One of my favorite and wealthiest young clients, Phillip, once told me he was going to purchase a yacht. Actually a ship. He already owed several mansions in different states, a ranch in Colorado, and a beach house in Turks and Caicos. Why consider purchasing a 248-foot yacht with a crew of twenty-four? He just woke up one morning and decided it might be fun. Granted most of us can't dream that large, but it's all relative. We wake up thinking about a new barbecue. The old one works fine, but the new one is on sale for $500 and has LED lighting inside to see the meat. Mine doesn't have that. (I guess flashlights are passé?)

I pondered his decision to purchase the yacht and said to him, "Why don't you try *not* having a yacht?"

He looked queerly at me and said, "That doesn't sound very entertaining. I can't sail to remote islands with *nothing*," he said.

But I was serious.

He quickly turned to me and demanded, "Alright, tell me something *you* dream about. What is something you *really* would like to do or have?"

My answer was immediate because I had wanted it for so long. "You know that brand new jet black Ferrari Italia Coupe in your garage you never drive? I dream about taking the top down, putting my wife in the passenger seat, and cruising up the Pacific Coast Highway from Southern California to Monterey! I can smell the salt air," I said as I breathed in deeply. "I can hear the deep-throated rumble of the engine winding out in third gear." Without saying a word, he turned and headed for the door to his eight-car garage. He returned in minutes with the keys to the Ferrari.

"Take it!" he said as he put the keys in my hand. "Take it for a month!" He could hardly contain himself. "I never drive it anyway. It will be good for the car."

I grabbed his hand and slapped the keys back in his palm. "Thank you very much . . . but I can't."

But he did not become a billionaire by taking "no" for an answer.

"Then I'll flatbed the Ferrari over to your house tomorrow and drop it off. No argument!"

"If you do that," I responded cautiously, "I'll flatbed it right back to your house."

He shook his head in disgust and asked, "Why would you do that? What's the matter with you? Don't you see this is a gift?"

I did not hesitate to answer: "I've dreamed of driving your car every day for fourteen months since I helped you buy it. I see other Ferraris drive by and think about your car and what it might feel like. I can hear that engine growl your engine makes." My eyes were closed as if the car were idling next to me. "And you aren't going to take away my dream by making my dream a reality and then a memory. The dream is too good to wreck."

Now he was really annoyed. "I put you in charge of protecting hundreds of millions of dollars of my wealth and you have a major screw loose!"

What does self-denial have to do with helping your children learn to delay gratification?

Often *the wanting* turns out better than *the having*. If you can teach yourself that wanting is often more enjoyable than having; that the journey is more appealing than the destination, you have taught yourself a most valuable life lesson that your kids will learn without words. Teach them not to confuse wants with needs. If you help them appreciate the journey and delay the destination, your kids will be on the road to contentment. *Happiness* can be temporarily counterfeited simply by following cultural fictions to success. Do as the advertisements tell you to do. *Contentment* is a self-assessment that must be measured sober. There are few things more rewarding than needing less.

> **There are few things more rewarding than needing less.**

Walk Your Talk

Keep in mind, the two most important components of parenting are communication and credibility. To hit the bull's-eye of raising successful children, you need both a message that is accurate and a delivery method. Like a bullet and a rifle, the two are coupled. You can have the best message and fail in the delivery because your delivery is not the same caliber as the message.

Delivery is about modeling the behavior that confirms the message. Sometimes this is easier said than done. Children are keenly aware of behavior. If a parent speaks of diligence and staying on task but procrastinates with chores around the house, the delivery fails. If a parent preaches abstinence to her daughter but is seen at family parties drinking too much and flirting with friends' spouses, the message is lost. The most powerful parenting, particularly among teenagers and young adults, is modeling without trying to deliver a message. It calls for consistency. Your kids are waiting for you to take a misstep. It makes their excuse for deviating from your message easier. Don't wreck your message by behavior that doesn't match. And when you're in doubt about whether to put more effort into your message or your modeling?

Work on yourself. Build your credibility with your children. The message is the easy part.

I'm a 49er fan. Particularly a Joe Montana–era 49er fan. Don't ask me to name all the quarterbacks in the NFL. But I love the game. What amazes me about the 49ers under Coach Bill Walsh was his insistence that the player's skill and execution speak for the team. There was no taunting. There was no end zone smack talk.

The message to the opposing team was, *We will play the game with a mind toward absolute precision. We will take each of our individual skill levels and make them better. We will not accept compromise of our commitment to excellence. And we will NEVER quit.*

Jerry Rice, in his own mind, never achieved perfection. Yet he was the best receiver in history. No dance. No words. No bravado. Just catch the ball. His credibility was extraordinary. *Please Jerry, jump up and beat your chest to the crowd. Show them you think you're the greatest of all time! Don't let your silence hold the rest of us to a measure of self-control we can't possibly achieve.* But still no words. Extreme modeling. A historical message that to this day leaves me trying to remain humble every day.

My father showed similar restraint. He was a successful man. Through hard work and determination, he became manager and then vice president of Cadillac and Chevrolet dealerships in downtown Detroit, Michigan. In 1963, he moved to California to make his own way. By the mid-1970s, he had built a new dealership that supported around three hundred employees and netted him a couple million dollars in a good year.

My dad only took a salary large enough to support the lifestyle of a middle-class family. We were members of a local country club and took a yearly ski vacation, but for the most part, we lived modestly. My siblings and I shared bedrooms, ate dinner at home as a family, wore normal clothes, and had to earn our own money once we turned fourteen.

As children, we didn't realize Dad made a lot of money. Perhaps more importantly, the rest of the world didn't recognize we were one of the wealthier families in town. When people in the community don't know you are rich, they treat you like everyone else. That's a huge blessing. Other kids wanted to be my friend because they liked *me*, not my dad's money. I had a number of real, true friends.

But the fact that Dad took only a fraction of what he could have from his own company did something even more important . . . *it made him extraordinary.*

When he pondered buying a new set of golf clubs, which cost about $300 at the time, he spent months thinking over his decision. I remember him muttering out loud, "I better wait a few more months to buy my new clubs, until the dealership does a little better." His choices and actions reinforced a sense of the value of money for each of us. We didn't take anything for granted. He never once talked about the wealth he was going to pass on to his children. He used to say, "There's no guarantee there will be anything left. The auto industry can turn sour overnight!"

His words were prescient. Ultimately, the dealership was mismanaged and the family fortune disappeared. But my siblings and I were fine. We had our own careers, and we were each self-supporting.

When to Let Them Fail

It is difficult to deny yourself material pleasures when you have worked hard and arguably are entitled to anything you desire, whether it is a new set of golf clubs, a designer dress, or a 192-foot world-class yacht complete with helicopter and ballroom. It is even tougher to recognize when we are spoiling a child, especially when grandchildren arc involved.

Brian's grandfather was wealthy, and when Brian's dad turned twenty-seven he had inherited the family business of producing precision-machined components. Brian was twenty-four when he married his high school sweetheart, Gail. The first grandchild was soon on its way. The grandparents on both sides were giddy with anticipation.

Brian and Gail, like every young couple, dreamed of having their own home. But with Gail on early maternity leave because of a fragile pregnancy, and Brian's meager salary working as a computer programmer, that dream was unlikely in the short term. They were content in a one-bedroom apartment and figured they would move to a two bedroom after the baby arrived and Gail went back to work.

One evening Brian's father-in-law suggested the new family purchase a home in the area. Grandma and Grandpa could help out with day care once the baby arrived. It sounded like a possibility, but the down payment? Brian and Gail had none.

A few months later, Brian asked his dad if he would loan him $100,000 for a down payment toward a $500,000 home in a neighboring town. Dad keyed in on the word "borrow," and when it became clear this was a gift until the house sold one day, Dad wisely said "no." It was not easy, and his refusal caused a moderate amount of consternation between Brian's parents. The issue was thought dead ... for one day.

Brian's in-laws heard of the need and promptly committed to a gift of $500,000 on a $1 million home so Brian and Gail could stay in the area. An adjustable rate mortgage would ensure low monthly payments for two years of ownership. That enabled Brian and Gail to buy a new three-bedroom home with a small yard and a mortgage payment that was just a bit more than they could afford.

Bridget was born, and all seemed to be well. After a while, Gail went back to work, and Grandma began caring for little Bridget during the workday. After six months, Gail began to feel exhausted from working during the day and caring for a newborn at night and on the weekends. The infant was turning into a toddler. By the time Gail got home; made dinner; cleaned up the house; greeted and fed Brian, who was often working late hours; and prepared Bridget for bed, the alarm clock was ringing, and the next day was dawning.

Gail began to resent the fact that her own mother had all the quality time with her daughter, and before long, Gail insisted on being a stay-at-home mom. This caused marital problems between Gail and Brian.

After a year of stress and disappointment, Brian approached his father, Kenneth, and asked for advice. Although Kenneth had wisely said no to the down payment loan, his thinking wasn't as clear this time. That's because Kenneth had always hoped one of his children would take over the family business. So Kenneth proposed hiring his son as sales manager of his company and paying him at a higher than normal rate so Brian's salary was high enough to permit Gail to be a stay-at-home mom. Brian said yes, and everything was fixed in a nanosecond, or so it seemed . . .

Gail stayed at home, conceived again, gave birth to a son, and both sets of grandparents were overjoyed. They assumed their efforts had helped to produce another generation of a well-balanced family. Again, everything seemed perfect . . . until Brian began to realize he was ill equipped to sell precision components, had nothing in common with the employees, and sensed they resented him for having been made their boss without working his way up.

Brian felt trapped. His salary at his father's company was three times what he could earn as a computer programmer. His wife wanted to be a stay-at-home mom. What Brian and Gail did not know was that their parents were beginning to blame one another for leading the young family onto this ledge.

To make matters worse, the employees at the family business made it known that the morale was declining because of nepotism. Kenneth spoke with Brian, and the two agreed it was best for Brian to reengage his computer programming skills and leave the company. Kenneth agreed to continue Brian's company salary for several months to allow Brian's family to adjust to the decrease in income. Everything went back to perfect. Brian joined a consulting business known for programming and developing software. And now that he was earning two sources of income, he leased a new luxury SUV, complete with rear-seat video players for the kids.

Enter 2007, the mortgage crisis, and the crash of real estate values throughout the country. That year, Brian and Gail's mortgage adjusted to a higher interest rate, and the payment went up forty percent. Kenneth agreed to a reduced salary, instead of terminating the compensation as he had promised. The couple could not refinance or sell their home because it was worth less than the mortgage that encumbered it. Brian and Gail realized they could no longer make the mortgage payment. Kenneth pointed the finger at Gail's parents and blamed them for helping the two purchase a home they couldn't afford.

As was the case with many bank foreclosures, it took two years for the bank to take their home. Both parents thought it was senseless to help pay the mortgage on a home with no equity. Brian's family lived very comfortably for those two years with the absence of a mortgage payment. Life was a success once again. Brian didn't even need to work as hard because expenses had decreased. Then came August of 2009. Once the foreclosure was completed, they received an eviction notice. Brian and his wife couldn't register the severity of what was happening since the stressors of financial responsibility had never really fallen in their laps. Where would they live? They felt no panic.

Brian calmly approached his dad for advice. Brian and Gail couldn't qualify for a new home as their credit was destroyed in the foreclosure. They hadn't saved any money because they didn't feel a need to do so. Kenneth considered the situation carefully. He wasn't going to change his position; he would not help them buy a home. He remembered struggling to buy his own home. So would his son. "You'll have to rent, son," he said.

Brian seemed okay with that. But when Gail shared with her parents the location of the apartments they could afford, neither parent was happy. They thought it would be demoralizing and, worse yet, it would put them twenty miles away from the grand-parents. They had a better idea.

Gail's parents owned a second home in Laguna Beach, which was in a neighborhood twice as nice as the home Brian and Gail had lost to foreclosure. "You can rent from us," her father suggested. "The market rent would be double what you could afford, so I will rent it to you for half the amount until you both get on your feet."

Done and done. With the aid of a moving van and crew supplied by Gail's dad, Brian and Gail moved into the rental, and life smoothed out again. Brian's father-in-law was adamant the monthly rent be paid on time. Such was the extent of his conviction about teaching a life lesson. He did, however, paint, carpet, and landscape the rental before they moved in, and it looked charming. But within six months it was clear the expenses of the young family were too great despite the reduced rent and Brian's extra income from the family business. So Kenneth took the only action he saw feasible; he increased Brian's salary at the company.

Does this sound entitled? Who's at fault? If you are a parent you are saying, *My kids had choices. They accepted our good intentions, misused them, and have made their own bed.* If you are a child of entitlement enabled by your parents, you respond, *Mom and Dad, you are the adults; you should have known better!* The kids are right.

Had those parents modeled the lessons of restraint, had they not jumped in to provide immediate gratification in the form of a house down payment, high-salary job, and a salary subsidy, Brian and Gail would have had the opportunity to live within their means and the dignity to make it on their own financially.

> **"Mom and Dad, you are the adults; you should have known better!"**

———

Delayed gratification often requires struggling. Parents, like the ones described in this chapter, often do a poor job of allowing their children to struggle. If parents don't show restraint, their kids won't have a chance.

CHAPTER 5

DO Let Your Kids Struggle

ALLOW YOUR CHILDREN TO SUFFER WHEN THERE IS A LESSON TO be learned or personal growth to be had. If they haven't earned it, they won't learn it! Welcome their pain of life and witness them as they react and grow. Encourage them. Assure them they will survive, like you did. It will not be fun. But who said every step of this journey was supposed to be fun?

> *If they haven't earned it, they won't learn it!*

Consider Jerry Moretti. At the age of fourteen, Quirino "Jerry" Moretti completed the last leg of a seventeen-day trip from Italy to New York to Los Angeles. The year was 1950. Jerry spoke no English but carried a handwritten note from his parents that said they wanted him to immigrate to the United States and begin a new life in California. Mama and Papa Moretti hoped to give Jerry the freedom to grow beyond the small farm in Italy where his family had worked for generations.

So Jerry went to live with his Aunt Amelia, a distant relative. During the next ten years, he remained in the United States, keeping a wood-framed picture of the family on the farm in

Potenza, Italy, as the only reminder of what he had left behind. Jerry had known three things on the farm—hard work, meals with laughter, and respect for his parents. And now it was up to him to fulfill their faith in him.

By age fifteen, Jerry secured his first job in the United States as a gas station attendant. Then he began his climb, rising to gas station manager at nineteen, and gas station *owner* at age twenty-six. With his earnings, over the next ten years, Jerry began investing in apartment houses, mobile home parks, industrial buildings, land, and fast-food restaurants. He knew the meaning of hard work, sacrifice, and delayed gratification.

Even as his earnings increased, he remained frugal. He took sack lunches to work his entire life. His wife, Barbara, was also thrifty. They raised their three boys on a strict budget. They lived in a two-bedroom house long after they could afford a bigger one. They drove one used car. Their children went to public schools. Jerry purchased things only when he could pay cash. Credit, he remembered vividly, nearly took the family farm in Italy. He took no money from his investments until the mortgage on each property was paid in full.

At the time this book was published, Jerry was eighty. He and Barbara still live in the small home in Whittier, California, that they bought forty-four years ago. They have a cottage on a nearby lake, and a cabin in the local mountains, but both are modest and speak little of material success. Their children are grown, have families, and are financially independent. The kids don't ask who is getting the money when Jerry and Barbara die.

"So," you might ask, "what good is his money? He could have had anything he wanted! He missed out on so many things money could buy!" If you met him only once, you'd know he didn't miss out on anything. In fact, if you asked him about it, this slight, silver-haired man would put his hand gently on your shoulder, smile with joy, and say in his Italian accent, "But I did get everything I wanted . . . the freedom to choose my passion and work toward it my whole life. My parents loved me enough to sacrifice their family memories to help me forge mine."

Raising Eagles

Jerry's parents did what eagles do routinely. An eagle pushes its newly born young from a cliff-side nest. The baby eaglet plummets toward the ground. If the eaglet wants to fly, it does. If it doesn't, just before the baby hits the rocks below, the mother eagle swoops underneath, catches the bird in her mouth, and saves it from a certain death. She flies upward toward the nest, and just as she reaches the safe proximity of the nest, the mother eagle drops the eaglet again in a free fall toward the rocks below.

How close do you let your kids come to the rocks? How often do you pick them up, calm in the knowledge that they'll eventually learn what they need to learn and be able to fly on their own? Do you drop them again? Or do you return them to the safety of the nest? Having them securely in the nest is easier, isn't it? *At least for you.*

The tendency of modern parents is to hover. And overprotect. I saw this one morning as I was walking through the hills of Laguna Beach, California. I passed five elementary school bus stops in a span of one mile. At each corner a group of students was waiting for the bus. Each of these children had a mother or father standing with them. Most of the parents were holding their child in a tight embrace. Many of the children were holding on to Mom or Dad, too. My initial thought was *what dedicated and loving parents.* To one mom hugging her daughter, I said out loud, "Let's hear it for dedicated moms!" She smiled.

Then I suddenly recalled myself at six years old. I was living in Birmingham, Michigan, and my mom would send me off to Valley Woods Elementary School, on foot, sometimes alone, or with my nine-year-old brother, Tom. It was three miles away! Yet, my parents loved me. I'm sure of it. On some days my brother would stay late after school for projects, and I would walk home alone. Part of that journey was through a densely wooded forest.

You might argue, "Things are different now! More dangerous," you would say, "My child might get injured, or encounter a pedophile." A horrible thought. What if you took your child to the bus stop and dropped her off without waiting? What prevents you? Is it the guilt you would feel if your child was kidnapped or molested at the bus stop? Those fears are indeed compelling. Many people would agree your course of action is most likely smarter and wiser. But I'm suggesting your concerns might be partly imaginary and contrived, and intensified by fear and paranoia. There is risk in everything we do. The eagle risks not catching the eaglet before it is dashed on the rocks. At some point, for the benefit of your child's maturity and growth, you must take a risk.

Codependent parents envision every possible combination of failures to justify setting a course to steer clear of hazards. Most of the imagined failures aren't even remote possibilities. It fills your time, doesn't it! Try more effective parenting; invite the risk!

Looking back at my experience at Valley Woods Elementary School, I wonder how things would have been different if my mom had driven me to school every day, or stood on a street corner hugging me, waiting for the bus to arrive. What did I learn walking to school with my brother every morning? First, I learned a sense of adventure. In the winter, the wooded area near my house was a carpet of untouched white snow, sometimes powdery and deep. Once I had to dig out my tennis shoe when it came off in the snow! Heaven forbid the thought of your child losing his shoe and standing barefoot in the snow-covered woods. Even for two minutes. That's child endangerment, right? Pneumonia or frostbite for sure! Perhaps your child would be lost and barefoot in the snow while the search and rescue continued tirelessly into the night looking for your child while your friends watched on the evening news and stapled posters to every telephone pole. But probably not!

How long was my foot bare in the snow? Two seconds! My foot nearly froze. The next time, I insisted on wearing my snow boots and carrying my sneakers in my pack. Imagine such experience in a six-year-old boy! On a different day, on the path home from school, there was teenager who sold candy every afternoon in his garage. Right then and there, I became addicted to red licorice vines. I also gained a skill at negotiating and bargaining with the young man to get an extra piece of licorice. My older brother, Tom, showed me how an experienced nine-year-old could negotiate TWO extra pieces of licorice with the purchase of only ten. I picked up knowledge of pricing and discovered older people are generally more experienced and wiser. Older people are a good resource. I was learning.

One afternoon walking home, I met Jenny. We talked. She was different. She laughed funny. I liked her. She became my first crush. One Saturday I walked the mile to her house with a Christmas gift—a glass vase of bubble bath. Just as she opened the door, the gift fell through the water-soaked wrapping paper and shattered on her front porch. When I arrived home, the tears on my face had frozen from the winter cold.

And when my brother broke his arm from a fall against a street curb, I gathered people to stay with him as I ran all the way home for help. Just think; I gained all this experience from a walk to and from elementary school. My mom and dad were not codependent. They were strong enough to let me experience my life as it came to *me*. They took calculated risks and permitted me to take risks, despite the possibility of my failure.

There is risk in child raising. Don't drop your eight-year-old off in the desert with a quart of water and a bowie knife. But consider the real risk of allowing your child to discover certain things for herself. When they slip, skin, and bloody their knee, show them how to clean and dress a wound and encourage them to fail again. Don't weld emotional training wheels onto your child. You may prevent a fall, but your kid will never tour the countryside and will only know the confines of your own cul-de-sac.

When It Hurts to Watch

When I think about how an individual life is forged, I often think about the Italian sculptor, Michelangelo. He was once asked how he could possibly envision a great masterpiece such as the iconic *David* statue before it was born from a massive hunk of marble. Michelangelo replied, "David was inside the rock all along. My only job was to remove the unnecessary rock from around him so he could escape."

Every time Michelangelo swung his mallet at the marble block, a piece of stone flew off, and *David* was one chip closer to emerging. It took thousands of swings, each seeming to injure the stone, with debris shooting in every direction. Life is like that. It is a mallet that is constantly pounding on us. The pounding begins when we are very young. And it shapes us.

Can you imagine what *David* would look like if Michelangelo had been afraid to use force? What if people who watched Michelangelo as he worked had thought he was being destructive and messy? What if they had asked him to stop? "What in the world are you doing?" they might have demanded. "How do you know you are placing the chisel in the correct position? Don't you see you are ruining a perfectly good piece of marble?"

Michelangelo would have pleaded, "*David* is inside. He will be magnificent. He must escape! The only way that will happen is to free him from the debris and rock that imprisons him."

When we entitle our children, we pull the chisel out of the master's hand and tell him the block of stone is unique enough. *It's too painful to watch the confusion and indecision. It makes us remember our own pain of growing up*, we would say. *I know how that feels and I can't let someone I love experience that! I can't go through that again!*

Much good is forged from struggle. Try to remember what you consider to be your strongest convictions. Is it about spending quality time with friends? Is it about going out partying and drinking too much at a bar? Is it about not wasting peanut butter at the bottom of an almost empty jar? Is it about not cheating on your spouse? Chances are, your strongest convictions come from struggle or pain somewhere in your past. Did a parent continually embarrass you? Were you told in eighth-grade math, "You're stupid"? Did a boss make you do things the hard way, just because it was his way? Can you remember the feeling of a chisel and a mallet teaching you something you might never have learned any other way?

Sometimes, however, we remember our struggles and vow to ourselves that we will protect our kids from going through the same experiences, at all costs. Maybe we use what our parents did, or didn't do, as the focal point of how we are going to raise and treat *our* kids. If you feel you are a well-adjusted, competent, mature adult, then perhaps your parents got it right, even though you may feel some of the lessons were too tough. The important part is to listen and observe carefully. This is not a short-term

The best way to set your kids up for future success is to support them, not save them, in overcoming early struggles.

task. It's like being the pastor or rabbi to a congregation. You never get to stop teaching, and you are always being watched.

Do NOT make those struggles disappear. In fact, when in doubt, the action that will cause your child to struggle the most should win. Don't pay for your kid's spring break to Florida. Forget the new car at sixteen. Forget private school. Make them get a job to earn that trip to Europe. The best way to set your kids up for future success is to support them, not save them, in overcoming early struggles.

Just Say "No"

Remember when your parents used to say "No!" to some of your requests? One day you would ask Dad to use the car and he would say yes, and the next day he would say no. There was rarely a reason why the answer today was no. And if you asked for an explanation of why not, your dad would say, "Because I said NO!" When did we decide our children were entitled to cross-examine our decisions and that if we couldn't outwit them, we should acquiesce because logic should always prevail? The only thing a parent receives for yielding to the greater wisdom of a sixteen-year-old is disrespect and an entitled child. Sometimes "no" is like swinging a mallet and wielding a chisel.

One of America's most talented pastors, DeForest "Buster" Soaries Jr., once told me his college son called after midnight from his dorm room and asked if Dad could pay for a couple of pizzas for him and some friends who were hanging out together.

For most of us, this would be an automatic "Yes!" His son was a fine, responsible student.

Instead, Buster asked his son what happened to cafeteria dinner that was part of the meal plan Mom and Dad already paid for.

His son answered, "Oh, we missed dinner, and they're closed now. And we are really hungry!"

Buster paused, considered the circumstances, and responded, "I'm not buying the pizza, but I'm sure you'll figure out how to get food on your own. From now on, don't miss dinner at the cafeteria!"

He hung up the phone and, after receiving a scolding from his wife for being too harsh, went back to sleep. His son didn't starve that night. Rather than learn the lesson of entitlement, his son learned several other lessons about self-preservation. Most important, he never called at midnight again asking for a pizza!

If your kids are made responsible for overcoming their weaknesses, they will discover other untapped strengths, strengths they never would have developed if a well-meaning parent always helped them cheat or avoid a life-forging opportunity.

Don't saddle them by insisting they use the solutions that worked for *you*. Don't even share those solutions—unless they ask. And don't distract them with material things that might only serve to help them identify with a group of entitled kids, or give them a false sense of accomplishment.

One way to help children become more comfortable with challenges is to share your own. We tend to hide our weaknesses and failures from our children. When the time is right, it is helpful for your kids to hear that Mom or Dad didn't get it right. Tell her about the time you hated your own mom for what she said, and then discovered she was right all along. Tell your son about the time you were seventeen and were rejected by the love of your life when you asked her to prom and how you cried all night. Admit you failed. Use your failure to teach your son or daughter what you learned from it. Help them appreciate the struggle they feel has also been felt by you and that it will be okay. And when they show signs of having crossed that particular chasm, confirm their own story of victory to them. Remind them of their struggle and their success. Put a few of those under their belt and you will prime their pump for self-confidence and attitude toward their next obstacle.

Parents Never Stop

My kids are all grown and living on their own. You would think my parenting days would be over and the tough times as a parent are behind me. Wrong! Parenting is never over. I remember, as if it were only yesterday, the day we received the news a year ago that our healthy, robust son, Russell, then age twenty-seven, had colon cancer. This is the same son I almost executed when he was in college for buying a cappuccino maker at Starbucks.

The doctors told us they had found a large tumor that would require a six-hour operation to remove a twelve-inch section of his colon and the surgery would be followed by six months of intensive chemotherapy.

I asked myself what I could possibly say that would give Russell comfort or wisdom. My wife and I were in shock. But the words came.

"Russell, you are now walking a journey your mother and I have not experienced. Each time I have been faced with a crisis, I have found the passing of *time* has the amazing ability to give perspective. What seems insurmountable this very moment will take on a different, less ominous posture in a few hours, and even less tomorrow. But how to handle this next journey is what *you* are going to have to teach *us*."

I knew better than to tell Russell what to do. Instead, I gave him a tool. *Let's just stay away from thinking too much right now and wait for perspective to kick in a few hours from now.*

Russell's response caught us by surprise.

"In-N-Out Burger," he snapped at the doctor. "After eating nothing for two days, I'm having a terrible craving for a Double-Double, spread only. Can I have one, Doc?"

Have you ever laughed and cried in a burst at the same time? Or tried to hold back a laugh at a moment of intense sorrow because it seems so inappropriate to laugh?

"Are you serious?" the doctor asked. "You are going to have to have surgery within the next week. If you eat roughage, you will have to drink all the same medicine again next week to clean out your colon for surgery. It would be better to stay on soft food. Not to mention you were just under general anesthetic and cannot drive for the rest of the day."

"I hear that . . . " said Russ. "But if my dad drives me, and repeating the preparation is okay with me, would you deny a guy a request after you just delivered such bad news?"

I could barely contain my laughter. It was the first time in my life I found myself laughing hysterically and crying at the same time.

Russell's two older brothers, Aaron and Todd, dropped everything as soon as they heard the news. They worked nearby and drove out to meet us. Twenty minutes later, we four boys were eating cheeseburgers in a fast-food joint. Doing something so normal helped the fear abate.

What I learned as a parent in that moment was that Russell was an adult. That this was now *his* story. And the best thing I could do would be to empower him to make the best decisions for himself. As parents, we instinctively respond to our kids as if they were back in diapers, no matter what age they are now. But he wasn't in diapers, and so I needed to approach him differently. It was no longer my role to tell Russell what and how to do everything.

That week, my wife, Debbie, and I had endless discussions about what we should do. It was not easy. But one thing we were able to agree on was that we must leave the navigation of this experience to Russell. Of course, we have done our own homework on doctors, surgeons, oncologists, and treatments. But every time I felt like telling Russell what to do, I replaced it with, "What would you like me to do?"

It has been inspiring to witness him take the reins and become master of his own life. Had I tried to control things, I would have made some big mistakes. For instance, I thought only family and a few supportive friends should be notified of Russell's condition before the surgery. After two days had passed, Russ came home and announced he had put news of his struggle on Facebook. My immediate thought was, *Tell the world? Make this public like you were announcing a marriage? I wouldn't do that!*

I caught myself and decided to remain quiet. Good thing.

"I've already received 334 replies of concern and support from friends," Russell said, "and I have over five thousand people following me on the Caring Bridge website."

As a parent, I felt I must be living in the Dark Ages. Again, I had to adjust imposing my protocol on Russell. This is *his* life.

When We Have to Let Go

At times like this—when our kids are really truly suffering—we feel the most temptation to jump in and try to manage their lives. We want to control the outcome—but we can't. Two of my closest friends, Nick and Belinda, had to learn this the hard way.

Nick and Belinda have a son, Cameron, who became a heroin addict at the age of nineteen. He is now twenty-four. Cameron is the oldest of four children. His mother has an advanced degree in music from the University of Berkeley in California and plays the cello with the local philharmonic orchestra. In between performances, she is the consummate homemaker. Nick is a former navy pilot who became successful in the world of supplying manufactured military goods to the armed forces. He built a company that has mega fulfillment warehouses in twelve countries and four continents. He is a self-made man, and he and his family live a handsome lifestyle.

Their expectations for Cameron were high; he failed them miserably.

When Cameron was charged with drug possession, Nick and Belinda retained the best attorney they could find. Cameron escaped the first charge as a result of good (and expensive) legal maneuvering. And that meant Cameron came face to face with only a watered-down version of reality.

His parents spent tens of thousands of dollars on a rehab facility and psychologists, but it came to naught. Cameron had a relapse. Then over the next four years, he relapsed three more times. He lived at home, stole from his parents, and lied every time he spoke. In short, his behavior ground the lives of a bright family to dust.

It was clear Nick and Belinda had done everything they could possibly do to rescue Cameron. Ultimately, after taking quite a beating, they recognized they were powerless to make anything happen if Cameron wasn't willing to participate in his own recovery. If you are familiar with the Alcoholics Anonymous twelve-step program, the concept reflects a similar awakening for parents.

Parenting is about recognizing the longer you artificially sustain a path toward *your* desires for your children, the more apt you are to cripple their chance at recovery. And, in a greater sense, cripple their chance at exploring the uniqueness of their own talents and passions. Certainly, it is unbearably painful for a parent to stand by and witness the negative consequences their children draw upon themselves. But we must not discount the positive lessons and results that emerge from the same experiences. If life requires a certain box of tools, and every individual has a different life, then we must not expect only our tools to be effective.

Nick and Belinda finally got to the point where they realized they were exhausted, depleted, and *done*. So, with much pain in their hearts, they kicked their beloved son out of their home and onto the street and refused him money or support. They realized their actions might well result in Cameron's death.

Cameron left the state and headed for the Midwest. For months, they didn't hear from him. It was actually a relief. Cameron called near Christmas and left a message saying he would be coming home soon. Six more months passed. No call. No letter. No word. They assumed he was dead.

Then, as if he had been gone only a couple of hours, he called from the bus station and asked if they would pick him up. With trepidation, they told Cameron he could not stay in their home. Cameron said they could drop him off at his friend's apartment. Two weeks later, he was arrested again. They left him in jail. Their hearts were broken. Their spirits again were black.

The judge, supported by Cameron's public defender, gave him a deferment to drug court with a five-year prison sentence hanging over his head if he failed sobriety again.

Impossible, thought Nick and Belinda. *The restrictions are too great, and with a felony, he will never have a normal life.*

They were wrong. Three years later, Cameron is working at an auto repair garage. He likes keeping his hands busy. He fulfilled probation. The judge was pleased. The family has adjusted. Gone are their expectations that Cameron will go to college. Gone are the expectations their son will lead a life just like theirs. Gone is a life free of worry about addiction and relapse. But now there is hope—hope in Cameron's eyes and hope in his parents. Their hope is only that Cameron will be happy; that he will have moments of joy. And those moments will be enough *for him.*

This ordeal changed Nick and Belinda. They journeyed from embarrassment to humiliation and from disappointment to disgrace. When they had hit bottom as parents, rather than give up, their mindset became resolute toward one point of focus: celebrating Cameron's life, as it was and not as they had expected it to be. It was now up to Cameron to pick a life path. They would not interfere again.

———

At some point, the eaglet will have to leave the nest and learn to soar on its own. And so will our kids. Part of the task of parenting is learning to surrender to the will of a newly emerged individual and recognizing their future experiences will be unique and often unfamiliar. There are only two choices for the parent: either try to force your child's future into the box of your own expectations or celebrate each and every one of their experiences as they arrive. If you choose the first, they will hate you. And if you choose the second, you will have the honor of witnessing their dreams.

CHAPTER 6

DO Give Memories Instead of Things

WHEN WE THINK OF GIVING SOMETHING TO A CHILD, WE TEND TO
think in terms of money or the things money can buy. We rarely
think about time. One of the best gifts we can give our children,
however, are good experiences that are so memorable they'll last
a lifetime.

Memories like these stitch a quilt of personal history that
strengthens our own individuality and makes life worthwhile in
the midst of a constant struggle. They become the subject of sharing, re-sharing, and when we get older sometimes oversharing.

But how many of us give an ounce of thought to planning
experiences that will result in great memories, beyond loading
up the camping gear and hoping for the best or calling the travel
agent and telling her you want something special for your family? We go to school to prepare for a career, we build a resume in
anticipation of a job interview, and yet we leave experiences with
our children to chance. Why? Although vacations may appear
as the likely place to have a great memory, they are often too
expected and centered on Mom and Dad getting away with the
kids. This is not a bad thing, by any means, but not conducive to
making family history.

Think of an experience you imagine your son or daughter would enjoy. Keep it secret. Then consider how, given your means, you can make it happen. Can you imagine your twelve-year-old daughter who takes dance lessons walking into the audition of a student who is trying to enroll in the Juilliard School of Dance? Interested in giving your daughter incentive? Let her talk to a freshman in the hallway at Juilliard. My wife did this with our niece. It only took a phone call, and this created a memory that will last forever.

What about your son who loves baseball taking a few pitches on the mound at Dodger Stadium? Doable? It took a lot of connecting, but my friend and his son had takeout food under the lights, on the pitcher's mound. No charge. And aside from the experience, what if you couple that memory with Dad telling his son, "Son, in case you forget how much I love you, I want to tell you again during dinner on the pitcher's mound at Dodger Stadium. You mean more to me than my own life . . . and I love you!" You want to plant a seed for the future when you have left the planet? Try giving your son a memory he thinks of every time he watches a baseball game with a packed stadium—a memory of Dad or Mom that will continue to pay him like a runaway slot machine—a flood of wealthy memories.

Make Family History

A private jet was in the air on its way to Orange County for lunch. The sole passenger was Michael, the president of Transamerica Life, one of the largest life insurance companies in the United States. Michael was in his forties, the youngest president in the company's history. He had read my first book, *Fables of Fortune*, and said he felt a need to speak with the author about the distance he felt from his own two boys. Michael was admittedly a workaholic, evidenced by his career achievements and meteoric career climb.

We had a wonderful lunch for over two hours. Michael conveyed his feeling of inadequacy in being creative when it came to how to interact with his boys on their level. I felt somewhat ill equipped to give him professional advice. Instead, I relayed to him the personal experiences I had created for my three sons and the secret things that were being planned in their future. I shared with him that my youngest son, Russell, and I were 49er fans and that we made a practice of finding a cheap flight to San Francisco every year to attend a home game of Monday night football.

Michael left our meeting reenergized and ready to add a few tricks to his family life. As we left the restaurant, he politely asked if there was anything he could do for me. My first thought was to say no, but then again, in three weeks I *was* taking Russell to a 49er game in San Francisco on a Monday night. My creative wheel was turning, and I thought, *Why not take a shot at the impossible?* Since Michael was president of Transamerica, it seemed possible that he might have it within his power to arrange a room for us in the Transamerica Pyramid, the tallest building in San Francisco. It had an unmatched view of the city and waterfront!

I asked Michael if he could provide Russell and me access to the Transamerica boardroom on the forty-eighth floor of the Transamerica Pyramid. We didn't have lunch plans for Tuesday before our 7:00 p.m. flight home to Orange County. Typically on these trips we had a tradition of ordering a sandwich at Fisherman's Wharf and sitting and watching the spectacle of people in San Francisco, something the mayor could sell tickets to. It struck me that a surprise visit to the Transamerica Pyramid with

Subway sandwiches in hand might be a $10 lunch extravaganza Russell would remember . . . forever.

Michael was almost kid-like as he smiled and left the parking lot to return home. I didn't understand what he meant by, "I think I can do better than that!" But I was about to find out.

A week later his secretary called and said Michael had arranged for our arrival and we should wear rubber-soled shoes. The morning after the Monday night game, we left the Fairmont Hotel and headed for the Wharf. Russell had no idea. We stopped at Subway and ordered our $5 foot-long sandwiches.

As we approached the Transamerica Pyramid, I said, "Russell, can you imagine the view from the top of that tower? I wonder if we could get up to the top."

Russell smirked as we rounded the corner of the building, until I made a beeline for the front door. I walked up to the heavily guarded front desk and announced, "Richard Watts," and nothing else. Two men in blue blazers and ties walked up to us and said, "Mr. Watts?" and to my son, "You must be Russell." Trust me when I say my son was completely bewildered. He was still processing how anyone in the building knew me. And by the way, I was already being elevated in Russell's mind from a dad to superhero. One of the men introduced himself as the building president and the other as head of security.

"We are going to give you a tour of the building starting with the underground terrorist protection systems, and then we will ascend to the forty-eighth floor." Both of us were mesmerized as we learned of the detailed security measures taken to protect the building from the unwanted. Most impressive was the tank-stopping garage doors that could close and lock in less than two seconds. We watched it!

After about a half-hour tour, we took three separate elevators to the forty-eighth-floor boardroom. As the doors opened, in the empty boardroom stood Michael, like a magician ready to perform his next trick. He shook Russell's hand and introduced himself. His title alone blew Russell's mind. "WHAT?" Russell squealed.

"I've got something to show you two. Please follow me," Michael said and headed for a stairwell exit door, up two flights of stairs to the roof of the forty-eighth floor, still forty floors beneath the dome atop the Transamerica Pyramid. The tower structure was metal and hollow. On this day, wind and a light rain misted across the inside of the tower.

As Russell and I looked up, it was as if we were looking up into the inside of a battleship standing on end. Spiraling upward on the interior were forty floors of a fixed metal staircase, which actually looked more like a ladder with open steps and a small handrail.

"Only a few people a year ascend this staircase to the top," explained Michael. "At the top is a small room the size of a Volkswagen Beetle. It shrouds a six-million-candlepower light called the Jewel of San Francisco. Inside the room is a guest log for the people who have been invited and dared to climb." Michael paused, and my stomach felt queasy. "My head of security will accompany you and Russell to the top if you would like to make the climb."

Russell and I looked at each other; both of us are terrified of heights. "Dad, I'm not so sure about this one. It looks slippery and a little dicey." It was Dad time. I knew if we could finish this story, it would become legendary. I was willing to invest heavily in this memory. With the head of security behind us, we ascended four hundred feet to the top of San Francisco! We entered the room, signed the guest book, called Russell's mother from the top, took videos and pictures on our cell phones, and returned down the ladder to the forty-eighth floor to the feast of our Subway sandwiches, accompanied by an adrenaline rush that took days to subside.

On our return to Orange County, of course I got an earful from Russell's mom and repeated admonitions from my staff about how foolish that experience was. But for me, I was forever elevated to Supreme Rock Star Dad, and that will live on when I am gone.

The next day, I received an email from Russell. It read, "Dad, I am still overwhelmed at the experience you created for me. I cannot stop telling everyone, including strangers on the street. I know you wouldn't spend the time thinking these things up unless you loved me more than anything in your life. Perhaps I can be that type of dad to my own son or daughter some day! WOW!! I love you for all you do!! Love, Your Son."

> **"Dad, I am still overwhelmed at the experience you created for me."**

I immediately forwarded the email to Michael in San Francisco with the simple words, "YOU did this!" I waited. Ten minutes passed. Then my phone beeped, indicating a reply from Michael. "I am sitting in my office, looking out the window, and weeping."

Michael took me out to lunch a year later. His smile was ear to ear. He had discovered a passion for creating and investing in memories for his two boys. The dinner on the pitcher's mound at Dodger Stadium? That was Michael!

Become a Legend . . . for Free!

Sure, the Internet is a minefield of activity a youth can experience without ever joining anyone or leaving his or her room;

however, the real-life experiences we can dream up are just as vast. It takes at least one step in the direction of making an investment in your own creativity. Be selfish. Think of an experience *you* would like for yourself. Then include your son, daughter, and family. It still counts!

Entitling your children usually stems from giving them things. Experiences are safer. Some of the best family experiences come quite accidentally. But your eyes must be open to recognize and move on them.

> *Entitling your children usually stems from giving them things. Experiences are safer.*

A year ago in December, my family rented a home on the North Shore of Hawaii for a week. It was different from any previous vacation because we were in one place, there weren't many touristy activities around, and we were doing much of the cooking ourselves. Our two granddaughters—Maclane, age three, and Lucy, age two—were at a stage where the beach and a bucket were all the toys necessary to keep them happy. Still, to this day, their one obsession is mermaids. They have wallpaper, dolls, toys, games, and bathtub scrubbers—all mermaids.

At our vacation rental house, the sand was just outside the gate in the backyard. Each morning, I walked with my cup of coffee out the gate and strolled down the strip of white sand. On Thursday morning, we had been vacationing about four days. As I opened the gate, I noticed there wasn't a soul on the beach north or south as far as the eye could see. All of a sudden, my whole body shuddered like someone had jumped out of the bushes. My coffee spilled. Twenty feet in front of me, playing in the shallow breakwater, was a life-sized glittering red mermaid! There was not a person in sight, and this incredibly beautiful mermaid was frolicking with the biggest smile directed only at me. I approached her and said the only line I could come up with, "I don't speak Mermaid. Do you speak English?"

Her response to me was difficult to understand because, as it turns out, she was from Brazil.

"Will you be here for a couple of minutes?" I asked her, dropping to my knee with my hands clasped, to plead my case. "My granddaughters are fifty feet away in that house, and you will give them their greatest moment in life!" I ran as if I'd seen Santa Claus. Maclane, the older of the two, was sitting in a high chair next to Lucy eating dry Cheerios. I snatched her out of the chair so rapidly the top catapulted across the kitchen floor, which got the immediate attention of my entire, sleepy-eyed family members.

As calmly as I could, I spoke to the family and the girls. "Could you all please follow me? Papi has discovered something none of you will forget for the rest of your lives." Carrying Maclane like a football, I ran across the backyard and hunched down next to the wood gate as my family gathered behind me.

I told the girls, "Papi was looking far out into the ocean this morning and making a special call only I know. It is a mermaid call, and it sounds like this." I barked out a sound that was akin to a cross between a humpback whale and a donkey. But no matter. I told the young girls not to scare her, and I slowly creaked open the gate and walked down the short sandy path. The looks on Maclane's and Lucy's faces will be forever etched on our hearts. They were gazing at a real mermaid. And we have the picture to prove it.

Camila, the mermaid, chatted with the girls, flipping her huge and broad red tail around in the surf. She asked if Maclane would like to take a ride on her back. We all gaped as Maclane straddled Camila's back and Camila swam twenty feet out to sea and back. Then at eight o'clock sharp an entire film crew walked out on the beach from Victoria's Secret and began a modeling shoot for an upcoming magazine. Camila was the star. We had hit the mermaid lotto!

When the shoot was complete an hour later, the crew packed up and began to leave. I knew Camila would be shedding the mermaid torso and tail. What a dilemma! Do I stay with my three adult boys and help her peel off her outfit, or do I remain a legend and tell the granddaughters Camila has to return to the sea as I take the girls back into the house? I crouched behind the gate holding my little darlings; the best grandfather on the North Shore and perhaps, at that moment, the universe. My boys didn't bother to take any photos as they helped our mermaid shed her skin. Sacrifice!

So, it's impressive, isn't it? The little unexpected pleasures of life. But does the experience end? Maybe. Isn't being a legend good enough? Let's file that wonderful accident and call it good. I didn't realize how much my family was looking forward to another week at the same house this year. So we rebooked the reservation for this Thanksgiving week. Getting a fresh turkey proved to be a little tricky, but that is part of the experience of tradition-making. Then a couple of months before the trip, I got an idea. An impossible experience I could make happen. *I wonder where my mermaid is,* I thought. *Nah, that is too far-fetched. But what if . . . ?* So I contacted Jon, the property manager for the house.

"Jon, there was a model on the beach dressed as a mermaid last year, doing a photo shoot. Is it possible she lives on the island?" In less than ten minutes, he responded by text: "Sure, her name is Camila, and she lives here on the North Shore when she is not traveling on business. Here is her cell phone number."

It took me a week to feel unimposing enough to send Camila a text, but I did it. And I included the picture of her and my granddaughter Maclane, hopeful she would recognize how monumental her impression was on our family. Camila responded almost immediately to my introduction via text. It truly felt like I had landed a text harpoon and cellular fishing line to a real mermaid! When I revealed to my Monday morning men's Bible group that I was texting with a supermodel in Hawaii, unbeknownst to my wife and family, their doubtful looks were questioning.

NO one was told of the plan. But the day before Thanksgiving, my granddaughters and I tied mermaid bait (a shell-made comb and coconut hair conditioner) to the end of a string and cast it off into the surf outside our beach house. The string followed a trail over the wooden fence, across the grass backyard, and into the family room, where the end of the string was attached to a dozen empty cans as an alarm. At 8:00 a.m. the following morning, with the house barely stirring, the line pulled, and the cans started clanging. The girls were ecstatic! No one else knew what was coming! The girls ran to the fence, and there in the surf, all alone, combing her hair with the shell comb still attached to the string, was Camila, their mermaid, back to visit the little girls she had met last year! Camila had liked the idea so much, she had insisted on participating. And guess how much this little venture set me back? Zip. Camila, an accomplished model and seamstress, even offered to make the two girls their own waterproof mermaid outfits. *The appearance is enough*, I thought. It is sometimes important to recognize *less is more*. A lifelong memory was dreamed up, created, crafted, and rehearsed. The vision was launched, the anticipation was energizing, and a rich, lifelong experience was created for two children.

These experiences, particularly the ones that don't cost much but require a proactive effort to plan and execute, are possibly life's greatest wealth. And the chances of experiences carrying negative effects for your children are minimal. So go bury a treasure chest on a beach somewhere, and assist your kids in following the map from place to place to find it. And fill the chest with a picnic lunch and their favorite candy, rather than the title to a new car!

CHAPTER 7

DO Wield the "Grandparent Weapon"

PARENTS, THE GOOD NEWS IS YOU DON'T HAVE TO DO IT ALL yourself. If you are lucky enough to have good parents who are still alive, look to them for more than babysitting. Let them provide your children with two essentials you may be hard pressed to give: unlimited time and unconditional love.

If you're a parent, consider that you are still experiencing on-the-job training. It takes a lot of energy to raise children, maintain the duties of a wife or husband, provide a home, schedule vacations, advance a career, engage the community, get better at your favorite hobby, deepen your faith . . . and do all of these with a smile on your face.

In all likelihood, you have to move at warp speed to get everything done. Your son and daughter need rides home from soccer practice after school. You have to get them back and forth to *club* soccer after dark, and on weekends to baseball clinic and ballet. On Tuesdays and Thursdays, you take your son for tutoring. Life can be a hectic race.

Partner with Your Parents

The children's grandparents, however, can be tasked with two important functions: *slowing the grandkids down* and *giving them time and attention*. Grandparents are the space between words, the pause between musical notes. These spaces and pauses are germane to completeness in the words and the notes. Here's another way to think of it: Grandparents are the exhale when everybody else is inhaling.

Grandparents are the exhale when everybody else is inhaling.

Grandparenting, much like parenting, is very intentional and must be controlled, by both the grandparents and the parents. The two roles are very distinct. Grandparents have a lifetime of experiences and have already survived setbacks and failures. Both have made them wise and street smart. If they are patient and loving people, the wisdom of later age can be a calming, credible, and secure resource for grandchildren.

Smelling the Roses

Parents are uberfocused on the success of their children. As a result, their children only know *hurry*. Grandparents can teach them *slow*. They can show them what it means to just sit with them on the porch and talk. There's no need to take them to an amusement park, or say yes when they press for that trip to Disneyland. Instead, show children the joy in togetherness, in sharing traditional activities. They won't know unless you show them. Kids aren't exposed to nonelectronic things anymore, unless, of course, those things help them with a resume for college.

The first time my wife, Debbie, brought our granddaughter,

Maclane, at age two and a half, into the kitchen and said, "We are going to make cupcakes for your mommy and daddy!" my *parenting* experience told me this was going to be a disaster! Who would prevent the mess? Who would clean it up? Wouldn't it be easier to put her in a corner and give her an electronic toy until visitation was over? Not to mention, my wife is a meticulous housekeeper.

I watched in horror as Maclane tried to beat the powdery batter in the mixing bowl before adding the water; the powder went everywhere! Not just on the counter and the sink but also on the wood floor, which had grooves! Then on Grammie's apron, then on Maclane's dress, on her face, and IN HER HAIR! It was cataclysmic! But my wife, who has yelled at our three boys hundreds of times for making a mess, just stood next to her patiently. Like the Grinch whose heart grew to the delight of the Whos in Whoville, they began to giggle and laugh. Then Maclane's hand went into the bowl and emerged with a handful of batter and slapped it on the counter.

I had to leave the room. It was painful. The cupcakes were finished, and when Mom and Dad arrived to pick up the kids, they were greeted with treats homemade by their own daughter! It was a hit. Maclane felt pride. Dad and Mom were amazed and proud. They walked out hugging. The house was destroyed. Grammie stood at the sink cleaning it all up, smiling every few moments as she remembered Maclane's first baking adventure.

Today, Maclane and her sister Lucy, now four and three, make baked goods every time they come to visit Grammie. It's already a legacy. They prepare, mix, and bake. The mess is much more controlled. They are so very proud of the results. Papi suggested a new line of pastries: "Baby Homemade Sweets." But then I realized, *take a pill, Grandpa. This isn't about money, profit, or you! It's all about them.*

Grandparents know how to do stuff. It may take a little cajoling to slow the grandkids down to try it, but it is worth the result.

The Precious Gift of Time

Giving your grandchild time means being completely available for *their* interests. It doesn't mean buying them stuff. In fact, for everything grandparents give their grandchildren, they take something away. Treating kids to a full day at the amusement park, or any activity that targets keeping them busy, robs them of the *grandparent experience*. The grandparent experience is about helping identify the children's own interests, then taking part in those interests. When children are young, they like to indulge their imagination and fantasy. Guess what? It's great to get down on the floor and play with new age toys using old age experiences. Your grandkids will stare in amazement as you act their script with their toys.

> *The grandparent experience is about helping identify the children's own interests and then taking part in those interests.*

I remember having terrific times with my own grandparents—simple folks who had very little money but were rich in family tradition and faith. I spent many holidays with them, and when I was fourteen, I got to spend my entire summer vacation with them in the same house the family had owned since 1841.

There were no malls nearby, no amusement parks, and the theater was twenty miles away. It was just a small Midwestern town. For dinner, we all worked to prepare the fresh vegetables, such as green snap beans and Ohio corn on the cob. The beans had to have the ends broken off, and the corn had to be shucked.

Guess who had to do this task for every meal? Me. While I was shucking, my grandfather peeled the potatoes.

We talked about so many things. Those were confusing years. Papa was a great listener. When I would discuss friends, he would carefully observe the description of each one. Then all of a sudden Papa would blurt out, "He really sounds like one of your closer friends!" How did he know? He was right. If I talked about my fear of what high school would be like, a concern too general for a fourteen-year-old to answer without further experience, Papa would calmly convey, "There are some things you can't prepare for. You just have to be confident you will be fine. Things will work out. They always do. Sometimes life will be tough. And other times it will be worth the struggle. The cream always rises to the top . . . and you, Richie, are the cream!" Those words were historical markers for me. They have stayed with me all my life.

We did other fun things, too. One afternoon, the next-door neighbor, Bob Trindle, offered to take me and Papa fishing the next morning. Bob yelled over the fence, "We have to round up some night crawler worms for bait. Come over at dark." Not at 7:45 p.m. Not at 8:15 p.m. But at dark. What time is *that?*

I sat at the fence from 7:00 p.m. to 8:30 p.m. trying to figure out what time dark was. Was dark different for folks in the Midwest? When Bob finally appeared at the fence in the dark, I was startled. Bob had two iron rods in his hands. He put them in the ground six feet apart. Each rod had a long electrical wire attached to it. After ten feet, the two wires joined into an electrical plug, which Bob simply plugged into an extension cord that ran toward the house.

"Plug that in at the house, Richie," he told me. As I tried to insert the jerry-rigged contraption into the wall outlet, I received an electrical shock that made me yelp.

"You can't be barefoot, Richie, you're grounding the current. That can kill you!"

Negligent neighbor? Negligent grandparent? No. Awesome experience and an important lesson.

"Run over here, Richie, and take a look," Bob insisted. Immediately dozens of fat moist juicy worms were breaching the grass between the electrical rods. It was nothing short of a miracle!

Twenty-Four Carat Love

The next day Papa and I were eating breakfast while peering out the window at Papa's prized birdhouse. It was a miniature Colonial mansion, complete with shutters and all. It took him months to build. Papa knew every bird by its Latin name and could imitate the birdcalls of most. His problem—grackles—a sort of black crow. Large and intruding, one would appear, scare all the other birds away, and eat the food.

I looked next door over the fence, remembered the worm hunt, and had an idea. With the assistance of Bob next door, I invented and constructed an electrocution pad. It was twelve feet by ten feet and had alternating wires one and a half inches apart in a grid across a plastic bacon tray. There was a long electrical cord that was plugged in and a lamp switch to turn the current on and off.

Two days later, the pad was carefully custom fit on the floor of the birdhouse, and the cord was strung down the supporting pole and across the yard to the cottage window where Papa and I would anxiously wait for a grackle to appear the next morning. It was genius! The thing was designed so the hot and neutral wires were separated far enough that a small bird's feet wouldn't touch both wires to complete the circuit and get an electrical shock. The grackle's feet were huge, however—at least two inches across.

The small birds all appeared early in the morning and were anxiously eating the seed. The grackle soon swooped in and landed on the edge of the birdhouse.

"Turn on the switch," Papa whispered as if the grackle could hear through the glass. "Not yet," I cautioned, "we have to be patient." I was only fourteen, but I had become the inventor and builder of the device. So many emotions were simultaneously sizzling. Papa was full of pride. I felt a very new emotion—passion. As I sat there, I was already considering the improvements I could make to the contraption. I was Thomas Edison, an inventor! Unique and one of a kind. Certainly no one has invented such a useful instrument.

The grackle took a step onto the grid. The trap was set. I looked at Papa and threw the switch. A pause. Nothing. I turned the switch off again, then on. Nothing. Grandma sat down at the nook as the two boys were fully engaged in their prank. She arrived just in time to witness a historical (and hysterical) event. The grackle's foot touched both electrical wires, completing the circuit and causing an electrical current to shock the bird.

The grackle fully extended his wings and began flapping them in complete panic. The bird was receiving a shock but was not able to leave the birdhouse. As the bird's wings battered the birdhouse, wooden pieces began to break off and fly in every direction. First the small hand-carved columns broke off, then the walls, and then the roof began disintegrating. It took less than twenty seconds. Years cannot erase this memory. Papa's prize hand-built Colonial mansion-style birdhouse, which took months to build, was completely demolished in seconds by a Class 5 grackle panic created exclusively by Papa's grandson.

The grackle flew away annoyed and unharmed. The birdhouse

lay in ruins. I thought my welcome had just ended. Grandma waited with wide eyes for the first words from Papa. There were none. His face curled up as tight as a drum. He took in a deep involuntary breath. He burst out in laughter! His hands banged the table, and he couldn't control his laughter. He couldn't breathe. He kept pointing at the birdhouse and then at me. And then he would start to laugh again. Grandma had never seen Papa lose control like that.

That was one of the best days of my life.

———

And my best day was possible because my Papa gave me the gift of his time—luxurious, unstructured time. And what arose from that time was discovery, passion, failure, reconsideration, humility, companionship, camaraderie, patience, success, wisdom, and love. Try to get that out of a video game.

CHAPTER 8

DO Teach Them Faith

DO YOUR CHILDREN SEE YOU AS THE ULTIMATE AUTHORITY? OR HAVE YOU taught them there is someone or something greater than you?

Giving your children grounding in a spiritual or faith tradition—if you have one—can provide you with another parenting tool. Spirituality teaches self-sacrifice, humility, and care for others. No matter your faith, these traits pull directly against the entitlement of your child. An enduring tradition that promotes timeless values can provide children with a system of internal guidance on how to manage life. But like anything else, children must see their parents applying the teachings and modeling the resulting behavior. The earlier this starts in the child's life, the better.

At a cemetery garden gravesite in the Christ Cathedral Memorial Gardens in Garden Grove, California, there is an inscription carved in the marble wall that admonishes parents about this most important mission:

> Prevail upon your children
> That they may know faith, family, our traditions,
> And the warmth of embrace.
> For they are both your seed and harvest.

Our kids comprise a significant portion of our contentment in life. They will either contribute to your world of pleasure and satisfaction for having become productive and self-motivated, or they will occupy your empty moments with worry and fear as you become an unwilling combatant in the fight to bring them stability.

The belief that there exists something greater than us as individuals is part of the foundation of our American culture. Such a belief may be as simple as instructing children to do right because there is something bigger we are responsible to—in this life and, perhaps, in the next. A subscription to the teachings of a faith can give your child a big-picture framework on how life is supposed to look. Such practice of faith often provides answers to questions before they are asked. It provides answers in the dark of the early morning, when serious questions can arise. And such spirituality can guide you when you are alone and no one is coming to your rescue.

Fan the Flame in Their Hearts

Vanessa's grandmother, Opa, used to read Bible stories to her when she was five years old. A devout Christian and simple women of faith, Opa recognized that Vanessa was a special girl with gifted talents. Opa explained that Vanessa's faith lived inside her and that her spirit was like a candle burning a small flame in her chest. "Always make sure no one blows that flame out," she would whisper to Vanessa. "That flame has been placed there by God and will always burn brightly so long as you are true to your faith and yourself." Opa reasserted this idea often, and when Vanessa was a preteen, Opa added, "There will be times in your life when that flame becomes a feeble flicker and risks being extinguished. Others will try to push you or coax you in directions you know are inconsistent with your beliefs. As the flame narrows, you must do everything in your power to guard that flame. And when you think you have nearly lost yourself, that flame will ignite brightly and give you hope and confidence that you are on the path, your own individual path, that is pleasing to God."

There were times in high school when Vanessa felt unloved and lost, but she continued to follow her faith and eventually would realign with what she believed to be her true course. People can be cruel, and her belief in a loving and nurturing God gave her peace.

But college was different. Nobody around her thought about their faith and the ethics of doing good by others. Vanessa couldn't stem the tide that was rising so fast, and she lost herself. The Pi Phi sorority at USC didn't help. And the attention she was getting became intoxicating. Thursdays started off as drinking day. Soon it was most days, and drugs were added to the mix just to make each experience a little more indelible. Vanessa had a wonderful and attentive family that had done most things right. Her dad was a big fan but taught her to earn what she had. There were no freebies in her family. Mom had always been there for her and was a good model of a loving but discriminating parent. Mom was no pushover. All had been right.

What has happened? Vanessa asked herself. *I'm getting lost in other people's idea of fun.* Weekends were endless parties hosted across the country in venues from Vegas to Miami Beach and Palm Springs to Mexico. Her on-and-off boyfriend Jeff was the captain of the men's volleyball team and as close to a Greek vision as could be found. She had been with other guys in her first two years of college, but she couldn't remember each one for sure.

This week was spring break, and she joined three hundred

classmates along with twelve hundred other college students from the University of Arizona and Arizona State in Cabo San Lucas, Mexico. The scene for several days had been nothing short of Rome. The mornings were spent nursing last night's hangover, and the day began with more drinking on the hot sand at around noon. The nights were spent at clubs dancing until 3 a.m. The next day it started over again. This week she and Jeff were not a couple. She was unaware that Jeff was rooming with a fraternity buddy and keeping score on a dried coconut tree husk of the women he had sex with. Chalk marks across the face of the husk indicated that by day five, he had already scored six times. Jeff was competitive, and volleyball was only being played on the beach during the day. Jeff needed sport at night.

Vanessa could escape thinking her parents might not approve. They were a thousand miles away. Little did she know that a male classmate of hers, Lucas, had snapped a picture of her dancing with a crowd on the beach, drunk and topless, which was now being viewed by Lucas's dad and his sales team back in the states. That night, Vanessa couldn't remember the whole evening. She had been drinking all afternoon, changed into some clothes as revealing as her swimsuit, and joined hundreds of partying students at Cabo Wabo. The dancing and drinking continued until her memory went dark.

She woke up in a hot and humid bedroom, wrapped in sheets that were sticking to her as she tried to gain awareness. Next to her slept a tall, dark, and hairy male. She had no idea who he was. She was naked. It was early morning but still dark. She first felt sick and then very frightened. She knew it was not the first time in college she had woken up next to a stranger. But it was the first time she had woken up and not known who she was. She looked for her clothes, her shoes, her undergarments. None were to be found. In a drunken panic, she pulled the sheet from the bed and wrapped it around her body, and she stumbled for the door, into the hallway, then into the street, barefoot. She could see the water and beach but had to walk toward it to get her bearings on what direction to head for her hotel. It was dark, and she couldn't make sense of the nighttime lights. She was still lost, outside . . . and inside.

She walked over to a nearby beach cabana that was dark and now deserted. She wedged herself in between two lounges and sat on the sand facing the ocean. She was as dark inside as the night, and deep inside her, a wellspring of emotion began. Her tears were just the finale to a rumbling of despair that made her whole body shake. She was alone, helpless, and hopeless. She was ashamed. She was no longer the Vanessa that anyone had known growing up. She hated herself.

And then, from deep inside, she visualized a small flickering flame. It was so small that her shoulders closed to protect the feeling that it was almost dying out. She remembered being loved. Opa, who had died seven years earlier, was in her mind, smiling and reminding her that she would always be loved. Vanessa recalled her grandmother's caution, "Whenever your flame is nearly out, you must do everything in your power to protect that flame. Escape whatever is bearing down on you and concentrate on growing that flame back to a warm glow. Because without it, your faith in God, and your faith in you . . . dies."

> "Whenever your flame is nearly out, you must do everything in your power to protect that flame."

In that moment, Vanessa hit bottom. And at the bottom was her faith. Her faith in her Opa, her faith in her father and mother, her faith in herself, and her faith in a loving force greater than she would ever be. And in the moment, for the first time in several years of descending, she began to rise. She didn't drink that afternoon. She went dancing but didn't drink there either. She had fun. It wasn't hysterical fun like the previous day, but she knew she had come face to face with the woman she wanted to become. Her recent past was on its way into her history.

Vanessa is now married and has two kids. She practices her faith, not just in her place of worship once a week but also in her home, in her work, and in her family, every day. She knows she can *talk* about faith. But her *walk* is so much more instructive to her family.

The Faith of Our Fathers

Our country has wandered away from its early roots in this tradition. Our founding fathers George Washington, John Adams, and Benjamin Franklin all believed in God. They often referred to God as Providence. In their minds, life was a less significant portion of that Providence. There was a responsibility to act in accordance with the wisdom of that Providence. Shortly before he died, Franklin wrote, "I believe in one God, the Creator of the Universe. That He governs it by His Providence. That He ought to be worshipped. That the most acceptable service we render to Him is in doing good to His other children."[5]

George Washington believed God was wise, inscrutable, and irresistible. If you read the hundreds of letters Washington wrote as general of the Revolutionary Army, or as first president of the United States of America, it becomes clear that Washington's constant prayer was to be right in the sight of God's Providence so that his actions were in keeping with the Almighty's vision.

---

5   Franklin, Benjamin. Letter to Ezra Stiles, President of Yale University, March 9, 1790.

Washington acted on the belief that he was accountable to something, or someone, greater than him. Washington never engaged a single battle without reflection and prayer on the question of whether what was to occur was proper in God's sight. After a battle was won, or lost, he expressed gratitude to his Maker, affirming that even in defeat, there must be a greater purpose. The sacrificial attitude of a pious leader gives confidence to those who watch his or her modeling and inspires us to follow, or depart. As a parent, what do you model? Are you a pious leader who defers to the good of something bigger than yourself, or is it all about you? Your children see that every hour of every day. It is education without words.

Granted, some religions have made a deity oppressive, judgmental, and disapproving, which has resulted in a movement away from belief. Still, there is much good to be found within spirituality. The Bible, for instance, despite the assertion it is divinely inspired, is an astute owner's manual for life. It has chronicled the human condition. It confirms great practices and condemns unwise practices. When you are doubtful about the hardships your child experiences, the Bible teaches simple wisdom:

> My friends, be glad, even if you have a lot of trouble.
> You know that you learn to endure by having your faith
> tested. But you must learn to endure everything so
> that you will be completely mature and not lacking in
> anything.[6]

If you believe in the wisdom of a higher power and teach that to your children, you avoid much of the nervousness of witnessing your children face trials and difficulties, because you are

---

6 James 1:2–4 (Contemporary English Version).

assured these obstacles and hurdles will gain them more experience and eventually make them better young adults. In fact, if you really want to help the process, instead of buying them a new car, find something that will bring on struggle, then keep your hands out of the project for a moment because a unique, one-of-a-kind adult is being created.

Admittedly, it is difficult to determine when a mature understanding of a person's faith replaces the strictness of a faith that merely proscribes rules and boundaries. But for maturing children, boundaries can be a good thing when taught with the wisdom of the reasons for them. Owning our faith is very similar to the hope we have that our children will one day own their own character and not be automatons in following Mom and Dad's verbal direction.

Is Anything Bigger than You?

It is easy to understand why many of us believe there is nothing greater than ourselves. Consider our technology. We have power and information at our fingertips. Our wants for information and knowledge can be filled rapidly and without labor. We have instant gratification. We crave more. We want less struggle. We have far less need of oversight. Why do we need to acknowledge anything bigger than ourselves, when we have and know it all? What keeps us from plunging into the deep end of materiality, headfirst?

And what might keep our children from doing the same, even if we ourselves try our very best to follow the tenets of our faith? That is an excellent question, without easy answers. But one thing I do know—it's worth the effort to try to help our children when they are still young and dependent upon us for care.

Is there anything bigger than you? As a parent, if you are a Democrat, your kids will likely be Democrats. You never have to say a thing. And it is never too early to start. Our kids were all dropped off at the nursery at our local church during our attendance at worship. It was their home on Sunday mornings. The lessons of a faith give us common wisdom and a framework that can be lived and suggested to our children. Belief in something bigger than ourselves begins to carve our understanding and our children's understanding that we have a responsibility in this life to do our best for our kids, for others, and then for ourselves.

> **We have a responsibility in this life to do our best for our kids, for others, and then for ourselves.**

Our children are our seeds to the future. But they are our harvest, too, in the sense that a well-meaning, ethical, and respectful child is the greatest wealth a parent will ever acquire. It is best to keep the faith.

PART III

WHAT *NOT* TO DO

CHAPTER 9

DON'T Expect Them
to Share Your Pride

STEVE SAT AT HIS DESK TRYING TO GRASP WHERE THE LINKAGE between his good intentions as a parent and the results of parenting his daughter had become misaligned. It was simple. His daughter, Kate, had been perfect. The oldest of three children, she had always received excellent grades, excelled at dance, and been respectful to her parents and those in the community. In short, Dad couldn't be prouder. So proud, in fact, last month on her sixteenth birthday, he wanted to reward her. So he bought her a new car. It wasn't a BMW, but once he put on the custom chrome wheels, her brand new Audi A4 looked like it belonged to a young starlet.

Mom couldn't argue with Steve. He was right. Kate deserved it. Her mom, Stacy, was also proud. Everyone got excited. Her siblings looked on with excitement and wondered if Christmas had come in May. Kate had no expectations. Her brother and sister hadn't either, until now.

Kate had never really given much thought to a car. Not a used one, or a new one. Several of her older girlfriends owned cars. Someone was always willing to drive to after-school events, weekend outings to the beach, and even to give her a lift to volleyball practice on Saturdays.

Her parents remembered how difficult it was for them when they were sixteen to figure out how to buy a car. Steve had dreamed of having his own car since he was twelve years old. Stacy didn't think about a car at age sixteen because her family couldn't afford it. She had to share her mom's used station wagon with two sisters and a brother. It was always dirty from being used so much, and Stacy recalled having to wash it quickly at the last minute to carpool her friends to their high school football games. It smelled like their wet dog, Shotzie. Sometimes, her brother would store his wet and soiled soccer clothes in the rear, which would give off a horrid smell. In the winter, her friends had to roll down the windows to avoid the smell. But it was sufficient. Stacy never really thought much about it and was not ashamed. Her family car was not a source of pride. It was transportation, basic and simple.

As a young man, Steve made a point to be aware of every used car left rotting in an extra garage in his neighborhood. He worked hard to save $2,000, and when he turned sixteen, he approached his neighbor and secured the purchase of a 1965 Mustang with no wheels. After long hours in his own garage, and much conflict with his parents over ignoring his homework, Steve finally wheeled out his "ride," which still had primer painted around the reworked wheel wells and a set of used tires on shiny used chrome mag rims. No one at school laughed at him. In fact, any guy with a car of any kind was a possible source of transportation for others, as long as the riders had a few bucks to contribute to gas money. A buddy of Steve's helped him paint the car several months later. The paint job wasn't perfect; still, the car was a source of pride. Steve learned so much through the process of buying and building that car. He wished he'd never sold it when he left for college. Today, he would trade his late model BMW 530i for it, straight across.

Steve and Stacy felt good about sparing Kate the car-related hassle they had when they were sixteen. They assumed Kate would wake up every day, look out in the driveway, and feel grateful for the new Audi sitting there. Steve assumed Kate would feel the same pride he had felt for his first car, and Stacy thought any daughter would be ecstatic to have transportation that didn't smell like a trash bin. Additionally, since this car didn't need extraordinary servicing or new tires, they figured she would like it even BETTER!

We Only Take Pride in What We Earn

The problem with their thinking? Pride is not transferable. Self-pride emerges as the result of excellent effort, especially when it leads to victory and sometimes even when it does not. This situation was different. Kate had not worked for (or earned) the car. In actuality, Steve and Stacy were giving this trophy to themselves for having successfully raised a precious and award-winning daughter. It was a tennis doubles match with Mom and Dad on one side and perhaps other parents, or even no one, on the other side of the net. Game, Set, Match! Steve and Stacy win!

Kate was not ungrateful. She just wasn't grateful enough. Why? Because it was just a car. New or used, it made no difference to her. Audi or Toyota, there was no difference. But her parents had agonized over not giving her too much of a car. They could have afforded the BMW if they pressed, but they didn't want to spoil Kate. They didn't want her expectations to be too high once she got the car. Hello? Kate already had no expectations. The first words out of her month upon seeing the car summed it up, "Oh my God, I didn't know I wanted that!" She didn't care what *type* of car it was. She did not run with a crowd of teenagers so entitled by *their* parents that she was conditioned to expect a certain kind of car.

Children are victims of entitlement. A victim must have a perpetrator. Guess who? The parent who gives too much is like the criminal who steals and wakes up the next morning unaware he or she has committed a crime. What's the crime here? Perhaps it's stealing from your child a life experience that allows your child to feel real pride.

It was no surprise that Kate didn't keep her car as clean as Mom and Dad expected. Why should she? It had no real value to her. She took no pride in it.

The other kids at school talked behind her back. They whispered, "Kate's parents bought her that car!" Of course they did. And why would that be an issue? Who cares? Other parents care! It's a parent contest. You can hear Steve and Stacy talking to their family friends, "Can you imagine Bob and Shelly bought Angela a new C-Class Mercedes? What were they thinking? That is so excessive!" What? Angela doesn't feel any more pride in her C-Class Mercedes than Kate does in her Audi A4. So who is keeping score on this? And once you start the contest, what is the parents' endgame? Is Kate going to get a designer prom dress and a limo to compensate for having fallen behind Angela in the material girl rating?

Steve and Stacy lament to their daughter, "You just don't appreciate everything we have done for you. *We* never had new cars when we were young! Our cars had jock smell and rust!"

Kate is not living up to Mom and Dad's expectations. "Why did they give me this car in the first place if they were just going to complain how much I take it for granted?"

The simple answer is you can't make your kids feel pride in the same things you do. They have to find their own source of pride. Maybe your son has more pride in having four gold rings in his nose and being able to land skateboard tricks on forbidden school grounds after hours. Maybe your seventeen-year-old daughter is proud of her double palm-sized tattoo across her rear bikini line. You warned her, she disobeyed, and it's done! Can you celebrate that? Children and young adults have to find their own mountains and set their course so they can take ownership of their own lives.

> *You can't make your kids feel pride in the same things you do. They have to find their own source of pride.*

There are no shortcuts. If you want to influence them, as I have said, walk your talk! Modeling behavior to your children is the best way to present a choice to your kids for their own behavior. If your behavior has positive results for you, they will copy that behavior. If they witness negative results from your behavior, they will most likely steer clear of it. The best a parent can do is lead by example and keep the lines of communication open. Stay genuinely interested, and love them for all they do—even things you may disapprove of. It isn't important that "you told them so." It's more important they learn from their mistakes. Remember, pride is earned, not learned!

Stop Enabling Entitlement

Dan was nineteen. He was still living at home. His parents, Robb and Patty, had given him every opportunity his entire life. It only took one year of community college for Dan to recognize school wasn't for him; it was too much work. He didn't participate in class, didn't do the work, and often skipped class. His professors were not impressed.

Dan's sister sucked up most of the positive oxygen from their parents. She effortlessly got most everything right. She was older and married with three kids. But dinner at home every night was organized around Dan's schedule, which usually included hanging out with friends and/or starting new entrepreneurial ventures with acquaintances. These typically lasted through two or three meetings—meetings in which alcohol and marijuana assisted in the catalyst of grand ideas. Sometimes Dan worked real jobs, but his tenure in them rarely lasted beyond a few months. It was easy for him to recognize most jobs didn't reflect his intellectually sensitive nature. Robb and Patty were well-intentioned parents with a penchant for good listening. Dan would arrive home late each night to the dinner table, and Mom and Dad would patiently listen to his "new" ideas for mega successful ventures in the future. Then Mom would clear the table and do the dishes, while Dad and son would retire to the television room. There, Dan would ask for his parents' continued financial support until he fully got his ideas in place.

Unbeknownst to him, Dan caused huge arguments between Robb and Patty. Each desperately sought the same thing—their son's success. But they differed greatly in their opinions of who was at fault for stalling that success. Robb thought Dan needed more time to develop his plan. After all, Bill Gates dropped out of Harvard and still created something from his ideas that was hugely successful—Microsoft. Robb also thought Patty mothered Dan too much and made him too soft. Soft and lazy. Patty, on the other hand, wanted Dan to get a real job and stick with it. And she wanted him out of the house. Their different perspectives on parenting fed a hopeless conflict.

Eventually, Patty convinced Robb to provide Dan with enough money for an apartment, just until Dan "got on his feet." All seemed well until Dan was still unemployed at the end of six months. Dan tried to convince Mom and Dad he needed to move back home for just a couple of months to get his bearings. Mom said, "NO!" Dad said, "Okay, but only for three months."

Dan agreed. He had decided to join the Marines. Patty was horrified. Her son could be sent to the Middle East . . . a war zone.

After six months of sidestepping, partly with the help of Mom, Dan joined the military and was sent off to boot camp. Dan was very resourceful during his time in the Marines. He opted for technical training, which meant he never would have to fight on the front lines. He turned out to be exceptional at writing logistics programs and was soon recognized for his ability in helping the military supply its troops.

Robb and Patty still worried as they followed nightly news briefings from Iraq. They were never sure if Dan would survive another day. They had to loosen their grip to avoid continuous anxiety.

But Dan couldn't have been happier. He had focus, survival skills, and a talent for BS-ing his way into any position he wanted. He also got involved in a serious relationship with a local girl who lived near Fort Bragg, North Carolina. After two years abroad, and a lot of Skype and FaceTime with his parents, he brought his new bride home. They decided to move to Phoenix so Dan could begin civilian life, working in the tech industry.

He left the military on excellent terms and genuinely felt proud of his accomplishments.

Robb and Patty felt such pride that they couldn't contain themselves. In fact, they overshared all the time. Isn't it interesting how parents who are disappointed in a son or daughter take such pride in the slightest initiative of that child? In this case their pride was deserved.

As Dan left the house for Phoenix with a U-Haul trailer behind his truck, Robb put his arms around his son and daughter-in-law. "By the way, son, if you have any other incidental move-in expenses, please call your mother, and she will see to it that you don't struggle getting set up in your new home! Just be conservative," Robb offered. "And allow me to pay for the U-Haul to get you to Phoenix. You've made your mother and me so very proud. Your new bride is so lovely and sweet, it's the least we can do."

Robb and Patty stood arm in arm as Dan put the last of his belongings in the truck.

"Thanks, Sir . . . sorry. Dad. We will be home soon . . . but not to stay!" Dan smiled. All laughed.

"Thanks again, Mom and Dad. Love you much," Dan said as he and his wife jumped up into the cab of the truck.

A month later, Robb received their MasterCard bill. Patty remembers the moment. She could hear Robb from his home office. "Patty! What in the hell did you offer to pay for? These charges look like someone is furnishing a whole house." Robb was fuming. Patty knew it was better to be silent.

"That son of a bitch. He stole from me. He didn't learn a damn thing. This is it. He can have his frickin' life. He has NO PRIDE! I'm never talking to the thieving bastard again."

What Robb didn't expect was the broad interpretation of "move-in expenses." Dan, apparently with the approval of their new daughter-in-law, had asked Patty to pay for the U-Haul, as

Dad had promised, and also gas, restaurant meals for the trip, a new living room couch and love seat set from Pottery Barn, and a new refrigerator. They also filled every cupboard with food and drink at Patty and Robb's expense. The bill was nearly $8,000. Interestingly, Robb did not stay very mad at Patty, because if his son had asked him, he probably would have allowed the same expenditures. Old habits die hard!

Dan was calm, direct, and not defensive with his father. "Dad, we didn't have the cash or credit to get set up, and so we accepted your offer to help us get in. Of course we will pay you back as soon as we can."

After six months, the debt was repaid. Robb and Patty finally realized the fault was all theirs. On the one hand, Dan didn't hesitate to take his dad up on his offer to help. On the other, Robb had given help hundreds of times before. Why was it any different now? Dan hadn't asked for help, and if Dad hadn't offered, Dan and his wife would have worked it out. They didn't need help. But once the offer was made, Dan felt no sense of pride in turning down Dad's offer, because Dan had never acquired the pride of being financially independent of his parents. If Mom hadn't kicked him out years ago, he would probably still be looking for his next pie in the sky venture and would have gotten even better at swindling people.

> *The greatest pride we can feel as a parent is to witness our own children feeling pride they earned for themselves.*

Robb and Patty learned the tough lesson that personal pride is not transferable. The greatest pride we can feel as a parent is to witness our own children feeling pride they earned for themselves. Yet parents are often the roadblock on this journey. When we enable our kids, we rob them of the opportunity to earn the self-pride that is gained by struggling and overcoming. It's better to love your children enough to feel the pain of letting them learn on their own.

CHAPTER 10

DON'T Sacrifice Yourself to Make Life Easier

WHEN A PARENT ENABLES A CHILD, THEY DULL THE CHILD'S experience, his skills, and his passions. That may "protect" the child from failures, but it also robs him of his success. In short, that parent is stealing from him. That is selfish and lazy.

Stop overindulging your kids! Learn to *stop* providing for them financially beyond the basics. Consider that a sixteen-year-old does not need a new car. That's a *want*, NOT a basic need. Rather than saying yes every time your children ask you for something, you'd do well to spend time helping them figure out how they can earn what they desire. If they want a new electronic game box, the two of you need to come up with a plan for earning it. Teach them the importance of understanding the correlation between making an effort and achieving success. In other words, have your kid buy it on his or her own!

Realize, too, people generally experience more failures than successes. Failures help point the compass toward achievement, and more importantly, they can become character builders and personality definers. Talk about their failures and the lessons that come from them rather than glibly saying, "You will do better next time."

DISCIPLINE IS A SKILL, NOT A GENE

The process of risking and succeeding, and risking and failing, teaches perseverance and self-confidence. The disciplined person becomes the disciple. Discipline comes from the Latin word disci-plina, *which means the systematic instruction to train a person. A disciple is a person who is willing to take instruction and learn the teachings of another, usually more experienced teacher. "Disciplina" was the Roman goddess who personified the notion of discipline. The word disciplina refers to self-control, education and training, knowledge, and an orderly way of life. The goddess Disciplina embodied the virtues of sternness, faithfulness, and frugality with money, energy, and actions.[7]*

Discipline is a skill, not a gene. It is something you learn and get better at with practice. Self-discipline is the assertion of willpower and reason to a course of action that often opposes an individual's personal desire.[8] It's hard. Targeting the best course of action while being tormented by your personal desire that opposes it is like two Clydesdales pulling against a rope in the opposite direction. The devil in that fight is separating what you know is right from your own motivation. But that skill of discernment, also, is learned.

7   "Disciplina," Wikipedia. Accessed April 3, 2016. https://en.wikipedia.org/wiki/Disciplina.

8   "Discipline," Wikipedia. Accessed April 3, 2016. https://en.wikipedia.org/wiki/Discipline.

As a diehard surfer, my long board is loaded at 5:30 a.m. three times a week, during all four seasons. Think of me like the characters in the movie *Surfing Mavericks*, only the waves in South Orange County are about four feet high (on a good day). Sometimes the temperature is in the low forties, which is near catastrophic in Southern California. As I travel south down Pacific Coast Highway, I typically stop at a famous donut shop in Dana Point. I know the Korean owners have been up making donuts since 3:00 a.m. They do this every day. They are ready to fill my order of one bran muffin and a decaf coffee. Total price, $2. For years they have been steadfast in providing the best pastries on the coast. The surfers all know the place.

Each time I drive away, it strikes me that no one can make a profit at such an enterprise unless they are willing to work every day, every night, and save every penny. Tony and Nita did. They emigrated from Korea in 1971. When they finally saved enough money to buy the donut shop in 1979, the two committed to a life of hard work. They didn't complain. Much of their motivation stemmed from the hope their daughter and son, Christine and Greg, would have a home and, if they worked really hard, a better life. Few of their customers realized they saved money that might have been spent on an apartment for the first six years they were in business. Instead, they lived in the back of their commercial donut shop. A makeshift shower in the kitchen area served as their bathroom, and their toothbrush and toiletries were carefully removed from the public restrooms before the first customer arrived, eager to buy hot, fresh donuts.

Nita was actually quite beautiful. But she was often absent a smile. It was my mission to make her smile. Usually I could do this by complimenting Tony on how gorgeous or sexy his wife was. As soon as I left the shop, I'm sure the smile slid from her face as she returned to the serious life of providing a better

future for their two children. Such lack of joy can bring on pre-
mature aging. They both appeared to have little joy. Fifteen years
wheeled past.

One morning at daybreak, I entered the shop and saw two
smiling parents. They were actually beaming.

Why? I thought. Tony greeted me. I couldn't order my coffee without asking. "What's got everyone in here looking like
Christmas morning?" With their usual very broken English,
Nita, in a high-pitched voice, said, "My daughter was admitted
to UCLA!" A big part of Mom and Dad's life mission had been
accomplished. And two years later, their son was admitted to UC
Berkeley. No shortage of gray matter in the donut shop!

All seemed well for about four years. Then one morning when
I stopped in on my way to surf, Nita approached the counter looking sullen and preoccupied. Her beauty was still present but worn
by several beautiful aging lines around her temples. The direction
of the lines made her appear sullen, because they pointed down
toward her ears in a frown, rather than ascending—the life scar
of smiling.

She knew I wrote professionally about parenting, and she
approached me for advice. In her thick Korean accent, Nita confessed, "My kids are lazy." She lowered her eyes in shame.

"They no like to work." She went on to explain how she and
Tony had given them everything and sacrificed throughout their
entire lives to improve the lives of their son and daughter. Now
twenty-five years later, their daughter had earned a degree from
UCLA, but only because Mom and Dad made her, and their son
was considering dropping out because he didn't know what he
wanted to do. The parents were crushed. Nita confessed that she
felt like the donut shop had been a prison—reminiscent of years
of unappreciated toil. She was bitter.

Sometimes it's easier to make a suggestion just to fill empty spaces in a conversation. Like, "If your house is too much of a burden, sell it and rent an apartment," or "If your marriage is tough, you should get divorced." You really don't expect someone else to act quickly on such a thought. But what do you have to lose? I decided to say what was on my mind. "Make them both work in the donut shop, and stop financially supporting them," I challenged. I was sincere about my advice. Allow your children to hate something enough, and they will learn to love something else more.

> *Allow your children to hate something enough, and they will learn to love something else more.*

Two weeks later, in July, when I stopped for coffee, Christine and Greg were serving donuts behind the counter for the first time since entering high school. They looked as if someone had sentenced them to hard labor and shackled them to the counter. I started right in.

"Well, Christine, congratulations on the degree from UCLA. Quite an accomplishment! And Greg, you are a senior next year? What do you plan to do when you are out?" Both kids were very slow to answer. They looked punished. Christine finally complained, "Anything to get me out of working at a donut shop!" Greg nodded agreement. And when I looked to Mom and Dad for their reaction, the light of understanding clicked on as Greg and Christine responded to my question.

Tears immediately welled up in both parents' eyes. These tears were so complex—like trying to capture the thoughts of a former veteran visiting the memorial cemetery of his fallen friends so long ago. Their tears showed satisfaction. Their tears signaled surrender. The tears meant as parents this lesson was harder on them than it was for their children. The tears said, "Thank you" to me.

Over the next months, apparently, things improved. Nita and

Tony realized they must relinquish control over their adult children and take pride in whatever Greg and Christine decided to do. The key was letting them take personal responsibility for supporting themselves.

One morning in December, I stopped in to buy a dozen donuts for the park ranger who mans the gate to the surf beach. Tony and Nita's children were off to new jobs they had found. They didn't know exactly what they wanted to do yet, but they were now motivated to find out. After Nita carefully placed each donut in the pink cardboard box and taped the edges, she slid the box toward me on top of the glass counter and motioned her hands to show me out the door. "No charge," she mumbled, looking away from me out of respect. "Our children betah (better)!" She and Tony moved on to the next customer, and although I wouldn't call it a smile, each of their faces had a pleasant look. Work was all they knew. It would have to be enough.

Let Failure Motivate

Intuitively, we understand. We learn from our own shortcomings and failures. The hardest lessons are often our greatest education. Yet when it comes to watching our own children fall into the same pattern, we reel with intolerance toward their course. We are willing to sacrifice their complete experience to soften our own anxiety toward the feeling that we are repeating *their* struggle.

> **We learn from our own shortcomings and failures. The hardest lessons are often our greatest education.**

The solution has been published countless times for over two thousand years: "We gladly suffer, because we know suffering helps us to endure. And endurance builds character, which gives us hope."[9] This is hope in something greater than our own struggle. Hope in our own ability to succeed and sometimes even just to survive is one of the most powerful tools a human can gain. It brings ultimate peace and confidence. Through your efforts and patience, things will get better. Parents who do not allow suffering in their children close the book on the lesson. In giving them an assist, they take away the prize. This is like helping your child cheat.

When I was twelve, I entered junior high. I was not tall, kind of skinny, and not very coordinated when it came to organized sports like football and basketball. But my dad had been the quarterback of the Poland, Ohio, Bulldog High School team, was extremely good looking, and got all the girls. Hence, I went out for the varsity football team. I knew the varsity was almost singularly composed of eighth graders, so it was not a surprise when all but two seventh graders, including me, were cut and transferred to the junior varsity tryouts. What I didn't expect was to have the coach, Mr. Fair, quickly recognize I had little training in football and couldn't throw, catch, run, block, or defend. I was demoted to hiking the ball for the offense, second-string junior varsity. I quit. Only three days of tryouts, a total of six hours, and the greatest failure and most important life lesson to me at that time had been designed, incubated, and birthed.

When I think of it today, I can feel my self-esteem leaking out of my chest. I never played organized sports again. I was on the varsity swim team as a freshman in high school, and I did varsity gymnastics, snow skied, and surfed. But my days of being humiliated in front of a squadron of peers would never come again.

---

9   Romans 5:3–4 (Contemporary English Version).

Interestingly, twenty years later, I was on the beach with an NFL receiver and threw him a football at forty yards with pin-point accuracy. He was shocked at my arm and wanted to know if I played in college. I jokingly said I had only played a couple of days in junior high. My parents never pushed me to recover from feeling such rejection as a young lad. I was and still am humiliated. I ran from it. I am still running from it. So, you ask, what good was the experience? Why didn't I pull myself up and make the team the next year? Or play quarterback? Anything to complete the story with a happy ending. Because I was scared. In my forties, I sat one day with my father and asked him why he didn't work with me, or teach me how to throw like him. "Because you didn't ask!" he replied. "If you had really wanted to play football, you would have asked."

"Don't you realize the humiliation I felt, and still feel, from that experience?" I asked him.

His answer still echoes in my mind. "Richie, you are a better person with a little humility. You are excellent at so many things, but you can't be best at everything." He confessed to me that he, too, had been cut his freshman year in high school and had to work hard to get chosen in his sophomore year. "You didn't want it as bad as me, so you chose other things to excel in. Trust me, son, it was difficult to watch you struggle when you were cut. But I knew the pain was doing its work inside you. It was exciting to be confident that it would bring out your best somewhere else."

"Dad, you have no idea how much hurt that has caused me," I told him.

"Good," he said. Nothing else. The subject was closed. We never spoke of it again. He was right. And that incident still motivates me to persevere in the direst of circumstances. Having survived that humiliation all these years gives me the confidence to know I will continue to press on, even with the pain of that memory. *Life is painful. Living is finding meaning in the pain.*

Some of the most accomplished people on the planet are people who have had to put up with considerable hardship. This is a worthwhile thought to reflect on when you worry you are being too tough on your children.

From Struggle Comes Strength

Consider Theodore Roosevelt. By the age of twenty-six, he had already overcome much. As a youngster, he had severe asthma, but through exercise and exertion, he learned to cope with it. Although his father was well off, other than family vacations, he was expected to climb his own mountain. He had done that admirably. During his youth, after Ted was severely beaten up by two kids on a campout, his father gave him boxing lessons. His father was repulsed by cruelty, shunned cowardice, refused idleness, and modeled truthfulness.

His father died when Ted was nineteen years old. Ted's mother, Mittie, had been his rock in his youth. She was his light. His encourager. He graduated Harvard, found a penchant for writing, and got involved in local government.

On one occasion in February, he was headed home to be with the woman of his dreams, Alice, his wife, who was soon to give birth to his first daughter. Baby Alice was born on February 12, 1884. Ted's mother had contracted typhoid and was staying with Ted and Alice at their home. Two days later, on Valentine's Day, Ted's mother died at 3:00 a.m. in their home.

With no warning, his dear wife, Alice, died eleven hours later of Bright's disease, which had been masked by the pregnancy.[10] Ted lost his wife—the mother of his newborn daughter—and his mother on the same day.

What does a grief-stricken husband, father, and son do with a new baby daughter? He left baby Alice in the care of his sister, Bamie, and he drew his strength from obstacles he'd faced and overcome in his past. He hid himself for two years away from the madness, until he was healed and ready to begin again. He had been empowered by his parents to survive his own life tragedies. He also formulated dreams that he resurrected when his vision returned. They weren't his parents' dreams. They were his.

Today, his face is memorialized as one of the four carvings on Mount Rushmore in South Dakota. He became the governor of New York and the twenty-sixth president of the United States of America. Few people recall he was shot in the chest by a would-be assassin in 1912. The bullet lodged in his chest muscle. He went to the hospital only after delivering a ninety-minute speech, blood soaking his shirt, and holding the diary in which he wrote the speech, the bullet having pierced the entire book before entering his chest. The bullet remained in his chest the rest of his life.[11]

———

In short, Roosevelt was a powerhouse. And that's because he wasn't babied; rather, he was taught to endure. Likewise, we must teach our children to endure and command their own destinies. It is not a failure to attempt boldness and fall short of success. It is only a failure when they don't try.

10 Alice Roosevelt Longworth, Wikipedia. Accessed March 21, 2016. https://en.wikipedia.org/wiki/Alice_ Roosevelt_Longworth.

11 Theodore Delano Roosevelt, Wikipedia. Accessed March 21, 2016. https://en.wikipedia.org/wiki/Theodore_ Roosevelt.

CHAPTER 11

DON'T Sentence Your Children
to the Family Business

YOU'LL PROBABLY NEVER GUESS THE ARENA IN WHICH
children's entitlement is the most concentrated. Care to take a
stab at it? Forget about family vacations, lavish weddings, and
all-expense-paid honeymoons. The answer? The family business.

Somehow, my father knew that. He never allowed his four
children to work at the dealership, except to wash the cars. We
earned fifty cents per car on the weekends under the tutelage
of Charlie, the auto-detail porter (and reformed felon). My
dad used to say, "I never saw the son of an auto dealer take over
his father's company and be worth a damn. All too often they
turn out to be insecure; be married multiple times; have spoiled,
worthless children; and never grow up!"

My dad's refusal to allow his kids to work at the company
forced each of his kids, at one point or another, to interview for
and accept regular jobs at regular pay. I remember working in
the J. C. Penney stock warehouse when I was sixteen. One of
the workers in the clothing assembly line—where the price tags
were pinned on shirts—didn't like me. He went to the manager
of the warehouse and told him I was stealing shirts. They frisked

me in front of fifty workers one week after I started the job. I was utterly humiliated. I thought to myself, *If this were my dad's company, I would have that worker fired!* But I couldn't. I was forced to deal with the employee on my own.

Through this experience, I learned how to confront people who talk about me untruthfully. I carefully developed a network of fellow workers who recognized my credibility and began to protect me from the disparaging comments of this other worker. Six months later, I watched the employee who had lied about me get handcuffed and escorted out of the warehouse by two uniformed police officers. The vice president of J. C. Penney called me into his office at the headquarters down the street. I was terrified. But then he shook my hand and apologized for the personal accusations and body search that happened six months earlier. He gave me a pay raise and told me he thought I had a bright future in the organization. What a life lesson! I would have been robbed of this life-changing experience had I been allowed to take a cushy job at my father's dealership.

Thanks to the work ethic modeled by my father, two of my three siblings and I graduated from college. Among us, we earned several postgraduate degrees and two doctorates. My father prepared us for life, both emotionally and financially. And that put us in good stead later in life, when managers my father trusted made some very poor decisions—decisions that effectively reduced to nothing any money my siblings and I might have inherited. Ultimately, it didn't matter. We never missed a beat. We were already working in independent careers. We had families of our own and were doing well enough to thrive on our own. Our individual incomes set each of our lifestyles. My brother is an attorney, my sister a teacher, and my younger brother a salesman. We were all self-supporting.

Twenty years later, all four of us are still married to our original marital partners, we have respectable jobs or own companies (in which none of our children are invited to participate), and each of our own children have graduated from college. Two of our extended brood have earned doctorates, and three have master's degrees. Not one is supported by Mom or Dad. My dad protected his family from the dangers of the high wire. By living below his means, he taught us to pursue security instead. More importantly, he never permitted his children to live a lifestyle they couldn't afford. Dad taught us to be content with what we had.

I wish more parents knew this. Parents who bring their children into the family business often blame their kids for becoming spoiled and for assuming they are entitled to more than they are.

> Dad taught us to be content with what we had.

But it is the parents who must take responsibility. If you have hired your child without thinking through the consequences, the fault is yours. You invited them to your banquet, taught them no etiquette, and now wonder why their elbows are on the table.

Before You Hand Over the Keys

Parents have a hard time recognizing that their motivation in having their children work for them is to ensure their children's success. The reality is these parents are failing to prepare their children for the real world of business. But why should they? These kids will never have to work in the real world. Right?

Consider taking a lion from the wild during its infancy, raising it in captivity, not allowing it to kill to eat, dulling its natural instincts, feeding it without teaching it how to hunt, defanging and declawing it, and keeping its environment comfortable and constant. What do you get? A tame lion that will never leave home. Why should it? If it did, would it survive?

If it looks like a lion and roars like a lion, then people think it's a lion. Give them a title of vice president or CEO, a fancy car, the right to roar at other employees, and what have Mom and Dad created? An employee who can't quit. An inmate of Dad's or Mom's zoo. Be careful, though. The instincts in your kids are dormant but not gone. When provoked enough, they can bite. You may find yourself wondering how your relationship with your children became so twisted and disrespectful. It can be painful and leave a parent very isolated and lonely.

Bridging a healthy (large) generational gap in a family-owned company takes skill and a clear program of advancement. The more enriching course of action is to let your children find their own passion and career *elsewhere*. They will thank you for it. If afterward they elect to work for you, and you allow them the control and position *others say* they have earned, it just might work.

John started by hammering nails. He was only fourteen and landed a construction job building wood-framed hangars for small private airplanes at a local airport. Soon John was supervising the work, then building tracts of homes for a prominent builder, and before he was twenty-five years old, he started his own framing company, which quickly got swept up in the immense growth of Southern California in the 1960s. He began developing his own projects and, by the time he reached forty, was worth millions, owned shopping centers around the state, and was in high demand for capital offerings from other rich people wanting to get richer.

His company was called Paradigm Development Company (Paradigm). He had the reputation, the skill, an exploding economy, and financial backing for the asking. John's children—John

Jr. and his sister Marie—always knew they would work for the family company. When they were teens, they spent weekends fitting into jobs they were made to believe they were doing correctly. Employees at the company all knew who John's kids were. They were hardworking and respectful kids. They deserved to be liked. But they were not. Employees do not like the children of the owners, particularly children in higher positions in the organizational chart. All employees who worked at the company interviewed and qualified for their jobs. The owner's kids did not. They never do. Even when a son or daughter works his or her way through the ranks, so long as Dad or Mom are active in the company, the kids will hoe a tough road. The general's son may have suffered through boot camp, but he is still the general's son.

Both John Jr. and Marie were to go to college, but only because John Sr. made it a requirement for them to work for the company. *He* had only finished twelfth grade, but his kids would be better than him. In reality, John Sr. would always be the best, but it sounded good, and it helped him act humble.

John Sr. was revered by his company employees. He was unquestionably respected. He had earned it, repeatedly. John really didn't care what the employees thought. Being revered and respected, and maybe a little feared, was sufficient. How productive and competent was each employee? That was his primary concern. Company productivity was his focus. He treated them very well. But all understood who the commander in chief was. It was his way . . . or good-bye. It was *his* kingdom. Many of them were more like family to him than his own family members. It made sense; they spent long hours together, struggling through the difficult economic times. This was the kind of struggle that builds company character, and those who had climbed that mountain with him were his comrades—war buddies.

Having a parent for a boss creates conflicts. All people hate their boss at some time. How do you hate and love your dad at the same time? Mastering the dual role of being the boss in one moment and the father, or mother, in the next is less difficult for Mom and Dad. They are not being told what to do. They are both the masters in the master-servant employment relationship and the alpha in the parent-child relationship. Being on the receiving end of these two very different roles (i.e., son or daughter first and then employee), often feels cruel and abusive.

John Jr. and Marie were caught in this vortex. Their family name was iconic and recognizable in the entire state. Their name appeared on donor walls and hospital buildings throughout the county. Everyone knew the names of the children before they were introduced. And because the community knew the children were handed their jobs, John Sr. would begin conversations about his family defensively with the statement that John Jr. and Marie had started at the bottom like everyone else. Everyone in the community knew this was not true. It is rarely true. Nonfamily members have to climb each step to the top of the company. Family members *take the elevator*. It's Mom and Dad who push the elevator's floor selection and decide how many floors the children get to skip. Why put your children in that position?

All Hail the Selfish King

John Jr. and Marie started with menial job assignments in the accounting and sales department. They did well there. Each reported to a supervisor who had been with the company for many years. John Sr. was still very busy building the company. He was too busy to take part in the kids' training. Periodically, he would ask the department head how the kids were doing. All was good. The kids were still kids. They abused their break time a little, but it was manageable. John Sr. gave his supervisors authority to be tough with his kids. That's what he knew growing up and, in his mind, would suffice for on-the-job training.

Things changed when John Jr., and then Marie, graduated from college. Each studied business. Dad said it was the best major to familiarize themselves with how to run the company. Young adults in college became aware of who they were. They were rich kids—the "Haves." To the extent the family credit card was communal, John Jr. and Marie fit right in to the college atmosphere. Each recognized quickly that their name gave them a certain entitlement. People went out of their way to engage them. They had celebrity.

When John Jr. returned to the company after college, his dad created a position not seen at the company before: chief operating officer (COO). Dad was still owner and chief executive officer (CEO). It was clever. John Sr. wouldn't have to fire or replace anyone to fill the position. The other employees wouldn't understand what a COO did, so it was supposed to be nonthreatening. When Marie graduated, she was placed in the position of controller, again a title not seen at Paradigm before. But Marie's position included the oversight of accounting, which meant long hours becoming familiar with payables, receivables, profit and loss, and assets and liabilities. From the beginning, for Marie, the job required both regular and extra hours, leaving her no time for a personal life. John Jr., however, traveled with his father, lunched with his father, and took up golf like his father. Their offices were connected. They shared Martha, John Sr.'s longtime executive assistant, who had been with the company for twenty-four years.

John Sr. often bragged his son would someday become

president, but he *never* discussed ownership. Paradigm was an intrinsic part of John Sr.'s identity. It would take rigor mortis and a crowbar to pry the company stock from his hands. The stock was his leash.

After five years, Marie fell in love, got married to a successful attorney, and became a stay-at-home mom. She was the lucky one. John Jr., one of the city's most eligible bachelors, was pursued by hosts of women, some more aggressive than others. He didn't know the difference. Brittany was crowned the winner. The community gossiped about her motives, and months later, they were wed in grand style. John Jr. and Brittany bought a home with assistance from Paradigm and garaged two sports cars, also complimentary.

John Sr.'s wife, Anna, did her best to get along with Brittany, but their relationship was doomed from the start. Brittany, unlike Anna, wasn't the kind of woman who would make sacrifices at home to do her part in growing a family company. Brittany did not know the meaning of the word "budget," nor did she show any desire to limit her expectations of the future. Whenever she wanted something, now was better than later. This immediately caused tension between Anna and Brittany. Anna convinced John Sr. to talk to John Jr. about Brittany. Wrong move. Brittany began to demonize her mother-in-law to John Jr.

"When are you going to get part of the stock?" she whispered. "Where is our security?" Brittany nagged. "Your dad could fire you at any time!" she protested.

The next many years were a struggle between in-laws, spouses, and father and son. Now add kids, the secret weapon of reverse leverage—an arsenal of pushback. Brittany now had a tool. Mother-in-law had better be polite and politically correct at all times . . . or else!

Meanwhile, Marie sat in the wings. She had a rather normal life with good relationships with her parents, brother, and his family. That lasted until the time John Sr. began discussing loosening his grip on the stock of Paradigm. John Jr. insisted he eventually have control. *No way*, thought Marie. Granted, John Jr. was working at the company and should get a salary, but not ownership! Ownership was part of the family estate. It should be equally divided.

Each of the kids secretly hired attorneys to advise them. That was a waste of time. John Sr. had no intention of giving up stock. He was willing to discuss it ad nauseam, but it was just casting bait. Further, the company was now a cash cow. It no longer took much of John Sr.'s skill and insight. John Sr. was getting older. He wanted to scale back. His ownership meant more now than ever. It was his platinum record on the wall. It was his Stanley Cup.

As time went on, John Jr. and Marie agreed on at least one thing. They believed their father was becoming senile. Not true. John Sr. took secret delight in the fact that his two kids appeared to be getting along in their conspiracy to oust Dad. He was two steps ahead.

Brittany eventually couldn't stand the conflict and left the marriage. She hired the nastiest divorce attorney in town. Brittany and John Jr.'s three kids saw Grandma and Grandpa less. Marie's kids lived nearby, and relations were good. So be it. Anna complained often to John Jr. that he should insist on the grandkids participating in more family functions. John Jr. paid no attention.

Three years later, John Jr. remarried Donna, who had two teenage boys from her first of three marriages. Her kids were not blood. There would be no opportunities for them at Paradigm. She was content just to be financially secure. John Sr. always mixed up the names of his new step-grandchildren. They were not important to him.

Despite endless meetings regarding the future ownership of the company, John Jr. could not escape his father's shadow. He was now forty-seven and most adamant about securing his future. John Sr. could fire him at any time. The power was all with him. John Jr. felt like part of a chess game. His father heard the complaints of his daughter and how she was concerned with the fairness of the stock being split down the middle. Marie's husband, a lawyer, had ideas of how easily that could be accomplished now, or after. After what? The king's death? Were they all now talking out loud about that? Like it was a historical event ready to happen? Family business is still business.

John Jr. engaged counsel under the guise of a succession plan and tried to influence John Sr. in being reasonable. John Sr. enjoyed all the attention. In his senior years, he was fully engaged. Not with the business, but with the naïve skills being employed by his kids to push him off the throne. The subliminal conversations—spoken, written, and tacit—were burning up life energy, yet John Sr. had them all trapped. It was his chessboard, his players, his rules, and always his move.

> **It was his chessboard, his players, his rules, and always his move.**

John Jr. talked endlessly to Donna about quitting. He didn't need this. He was losing his hair and felt stressed all the time. But where would he go? Who would he work for? Would it be different working for someone else's family company or a huge corporation? Could he afford the pay cut? He now had child support payments and spousal support for Brittany. The answer was all too clear. Checkmate.

Planning to Rule from the Grave

John Sr. finally devised a plan to let each of the two kids buy twenty-four and one half percent of the company. It would still give him control, but it would hopefully placate his two children. It worked . . . for five years. John Sr. continued to become less active in the company. His mind was relaxing in old age. John Jr. was there every day. Marie only attended the board meetings. She received distributions of profits for her twenty-four and one half percent. John Jr. felt cheated every moment of the day.

Then on a rainy Monday, during a board meeting, it happened. John Sr. was allowing John Jr. to run the meeting. There were twelve people in the conference room at company headquarters. The top brass of the company were there along with Anna, Marie, and the family attorney. Halfway into the morning, John Jr. proposed that his father remain the chairman of the board, which in a family-owned company doesn't mean much more than owner, and that John Jr. be elected CEO to replace his father. By the formality of the presentation, it was apparent John Jr. had prepared this move way in advance of the meeting and rehearsed it with his wife.

"Wait until my body is cold!" John Sr. blurted, legitimately considering the proposal a joke. It was no joke.

"I'm serious, Dad. It's time for me to be recognized for what I do around here," John Jr. insisted.

Marie jumped in quickly, recognizing the move for what it was: a gambit to gain control—positioning today, majority shareholder tomorrow. "Don't you think that's a little cold, brother?" she asked, looking at her dad. "It's Daddy's company, not yours. Do you expect to just take it away from him?"

John Jr. wound up and took a full swing. "Dad, you are making poor decisions, you are not attending important meetings, and *our* company isn't going to remain profitable if you don't move out of my way!"

"Poor decisions?" John Sr. said quietly, as if it were the only part of John Jr.'s comment he heard. *"You* couldn't make *any* decisions if I hadn't built this company and given you a job." The room was still. The nonfamily officers wanted to become invisible. They knew what was coming. "You see your mother sitting here?" He pointed to Anna. "She was here before I got my first job, helped me with the books when Paradigm was started, and has supported me through my entire career. Selecting your mother was a *good* decision!" John Sr. paused. "You talk about poor decision making? What about you? That first wife of yours wasn't worth a pot to piss in, and the second isn't far off. Not to mention the grandkids you have brought me are lazy and money-grubbing little bastards!"

Perhaps it was age. John Sr. couldn't filter like he did as a young man. The words he spoke, some of which even he didn't really believe, were used as a weapon. Keeping personal issues and business separated in a family enterprise is sometimes nearly impossible.

John Sr.'s comments were so outrageous, and untrue, that almost everyone sitting in the boardroom that day rapidly dismissed all of it as steam. Not so with John Jr. He sat down, speechless. In his mind, his father had just told him he was a bad employee, a bad husband, and a bad father . . . a complete failure. A nonfamily employee could sue for libel, but this was family; whether in celebration, battle, or outright war, everyone is supposed to forgive.

As John Jr. sat, the tears welled up in his eyes. He had taken quite a blow. Marie looked across the table and began to weep, seeing her brother in tears for the first time. John Jr.

stood up, gathered his laptop, notepad, and pen, and he left the boardroom.

"Where are *you* going?" barked his father. "Can't take your own medicine?"

John Jr. didn't say a word. He couldn't. He was ashamed to go home to his wife and try to explain. He couldn't repeat what his father had said. The words had done damage ... permanent damage. John Jr. called me, his father's attorney of thirty-two years. There was a porch at the law office, seldom used. That's where John Jr. sat with me and cried.

When Comes the Reckoning

The next day, I placed a call to John Sr., asking him to come down to the office. He did. We sat on the same porch.

"What is so urgent?" John Sr. joked. "Did my daughter call you to ask me to give her spoiled children a job for the summer?" He chuckled with amusement.

Once in a great while, putting your job on the line to speak the truth is one of life's jewels. "You and I have done business for more than thirty years." I said to John Sr., more as a statement of fact than a question.

He nodded.

"And you and I both know you can fire me at any time for no reason at all?"

"Yeah, but you know I would never do that. We've come too far together . . . unless you're sleepin' with my wife!" John Sr. slapped his leg. "Actually, that might get her fangs out of my neck!" Now he was laughing out loud.

"John. I have one question I've always wanted to ask you."

"Yeah?" John Sr. sobered a bit.

"Were you *born* stupid, or did you *teach* yourself to be that way?"

John Sr. let out a little laugh. "What's this about anyway? *You* called *me* here."

"Of all the wonderful things I have been part of in your business and family history, the successes, the setbacks, the lawsuits, the struggle, you turn out to be brilliant enough to blow the whole thing up in less than sixty seconds!"

"What in the world are you talking about? Is this about the stock thing with the kids again?" John snapped as he was beginning to get serious.

"No, I'm talking about stripping your son in front of the whole world and basically telling him you are ashamed of him. Did you even pause after what you said to think how much damage you were inflicting on him? You crushed him!"

"Oh come on. It's family! We were just volleying salvos about control. John knows I'm just punching at him. It wasn't any big deal," John said dismissively.

"Then tell me the last time you sat on my law office porch and cried for an hour over something someone said that broke your spirit?"

John Sr. made a few gestures with his head and shoulders as if he was having trouble thinking with his body. It was his age. Processing the unexpected was not easy anymore. If it wasn't in his repertoire of comebacks, he just bobbled for a moment.

"He's gone, John. You killed him. You killed his wife, his family, his job; you killed him. He has not only left your employ but your family as well."

John Sr. sat quiet longer than I had ever seen him be quiet. "You gotta fix this," he finally said to me.

"I will try my best. I'm just not sure I can. You will have to do exactly what I recommend, or you die without a son."

Over the following months, my plan was followed to the letter. Paradigm elected a new CEO and chairman of the board. It was John Jr. The remaining stock was divided between brother and sister—fifty-one percent to John Jr. and forty-nine percent to Marie. John Jr. had the right at any time to buy Marie's stock for a fair and predetermined price. Marie remained on the board so long as she had stock. You might think this caused controversy between brother and sister. It did not. It was fair. All knew it. Most important, it was finally decided. There was no more banter. No more indecision. No more chess.

John Sr. became a board member emeritus and was present at all company recognition ceremonies as the "founder." It was enough. He spent more time with the grandkids. He found he actually liked them, even the new ones from John Jr.'s second wife. They didn't want things from Grandpa. Just some of his time.

———

This story is not unique. It occurs often. It is not bad. It is just an example of the complexity of relationships when you mix family and business. It can be, and has been, done. If you doubt your family company has infection under the surface, go to your daughter-in-law or son-in-law—the spouses of your kids who work for the company—and give them immunity. Tell them nothing will be held against them for telling the truth. Now ask them if difficulties have arisen in their family as a result of being involved in a family enterprise. Sit back, and allow them to answer fully. You will be surprised. And if after hearing this true story, and being told your company has the virus, you don't make moves to correct and heal your family and business, then look in the mirror and ask yourself this question: "Was I born stupid? Or did I teach myself to be this way?"

CHAPTER 12

DON'T Share Your Estate Plan

MY ELDEST SON, AARON, IS A SMART, ACCOMPLISHED, INDEPEN-
dent adult. He is married to Rene and has a beautiful family of
his own. As an adult, he has always been respectful to his parents.

Awhile back, when Aaron had been employed by a small law
firm for a year, he asked me a question that floored me. At the
time, he was gaining legal experience and knowledge and was
inquisitive about areas in the law he had not considered before
becoming a law student. I remember his question like it was yesterday. "Dad, have you and Mom looked into minimizing the tax
consequences on your estate?"

In a mild amount of shock I responded, "What are your
thoughts?"

He continued without hesitation, "I'm sure you are aware of
documents like a family trust that can maximize the amount of
wealth you can pass on to your children when you die." He added
the tag line, "Of course, we all hope you and Mom live to be
a hundred!"

Whose Business Is It, Really?

The context in which I understood the question was this: Have *you*, our parents, been attentive to the tools available in the world of estate planning to ensure maximizing the amount of money *we*, your kids, will get when you die? A number of thoughts filled my mind immediately. *What prompted this question? Was he playing lawyer and trying to assist me in completing my personal legal checklist like I was a client, making sure all of my affairs were in order? Had he just discovered this topic in his own practice and was just being inquisitive as if he were giving me a tip on improving my golf swing?* Those were the only questions I could rationalize before the overwhelming sense of disrespect entered my brain. When did he EVER make it his business to direct me in my personal affairs, and where, in his rearing, did his mother and I fail to teach him the recognition of boundaries of what topics with Mom and Dad are *in play* and what topics are clearly *out of bounds*!

As I quickly drew together my thoughts and response, it occurred to me that it was time to say something that would leave a lasting impression. "Son," (this always meant something big was coming), "I know you might have good intentions in asking that question, but I want you to hear me clearly on two points. One, what we do with any money we may have when we die is your mother's and my business; and two, if you entertain me with a question like that ever again, you have my promise that if there is anything left over when your mother and I die, it will all go to charity!"

As the next few days passed, I reflected on Aaron's question and had the opportunity for some honest introspection. If Aaron didn't recognize his question was invasive and demeaning to me, then somewhere he had failed to acquire that sensitivity.

Or maybe he felt the emotional license to ask such a question. Where did he get that? I looked to my own training as a child and asked this question—Why would I NOT ask my dad or mom about maximizing their ability to give me money when they died?

A list of reasons emerged immediately. First and foremost was the cliché, "As children, we just didn't talk about things like that with our parents." Surely that comment made me feel old and outdated. Why? Because it was true. My parents did not talk about a multitude of topics with their children. We didn't talk about sex; instead, we got lectured. We avoided talking about drugs because my dad thought discussing marijuana might encourage its use. He did not want to hear about my struggles in high school and college because I was supposed to learn from those experiences on my own. He believed guiding his children through such experiences might soften their impact on the development of our character building. "You'll figure it out," he would always say.

When I arrived home one evening as a senior in high school in a panic because my girlfriend had missed her period, and she and I thought she might be pregnant, his first comment was, "Don't breathe a word of this to your mother. You need to look at all the alternatives." What did that mean? The discussion was closed. I didn't sleep for two weeks until the issue dissolved when she got the good news from her doctor that she wasn't pregnant.

When I was away during my first year at college, I sent my dad a ten-page letter explaining in effect that I was depressed, lost, struggling, and experiencing what I thought was the beginning of a slow decline in my aspirations to succeed. He called me from a pay phone at his golf course. "I got your letter, Richie. My thinking is . . . you think too much! Just try to relax. You will be fine. I have every confidence in you. Make me proud, son!" and he said good-bye.

Remembering back to that call, even today, I cannot fathom where my dad acquired such skill in psychoanalysis. It made me angry. And I remember hanging up the pay phone outside my dorm room and thinking to myself, *he doesn't care*. Figuring this out and living with my struggle was my responsibility. Eventually, I embraced the struggle and solved most of my issues. I now understood the perseverance it takes to withstand difficulties in life. It was a tough time for me. My dad wasn't ignoring my difficulties. He didn't love me any less than most good parents. His aim was to teach me survival.

Somehow, in raising Aaron, we must have taught him it was okay to make my business his business. He has turned out to be an independent and successful husband, father, and businessman. But parenting, like golf, is taking and scoring one hole at a time. You size up and execute each hole as it comes. Sometimes the game is easy. Other times you find yourself in hazards. Although a par is preferable, you are occasionally going to take a bogey. It's the final score that counts.

So what is wrong with parents discussing their plans of passing on whatever wealth they have upon their death? For one, it can give children a sense of entitlement to involve themselves in your life and in your affairs based on their desire that you not frivolously endanger their inheritance with bad investments. You may not believe this happens, but it often does. Second, Mom and Dad take on a value for their children that deviates from pure love and respect. Periodically, the concern over the estate obscures both the love and respect they might otherwise have. It is subtle in the beginning. But as the parent ages, it is common for these adult children to begin exercising control long before there is any real evidence you should release the controls to them.

REWARD: DEAD OR ALIVE

Try an experiment. Have a sit-down with your adult children. No matter if your net worth is $5,000 or $500 million, tell your kids you have made a decision to alter the estate plan and have decided to give all of your money when you die to a family foundation that must be given to charity. Don't say anything more. Just wait for a reaction. Here are the possibilities:

1. *"Mom and Dad, that's great!" "That is your business, and we don't even want to talk about losing you two!" "But we hope you spend it all and have fun!" Analysis: Successful child.*

2. *"Why would you do that?" "That could help our children—your grandchildren—go to college!" Analysis: Deceptive child. You have a stage-three child of entitlement.*

3. *"Why would you do that to your kids?" Analysis: A stage-ten child of entitlement.*

4. *"Can we at least pay our personal expenses from the foundation?" Analysis: You have a stage-ten child of entitlement AND a possible criminal in the making.*

It was the day before the big event, a destination wedding in New York. I took a short walk alone with the soon-to-be bride, Emma. She expressed to me how excited she was about her future. She had a good job working for an advertising agency in the city, and Anthony, her soon-to-be husband, was a new attorney, having graduated from Yale Law School three years back. Emma's family had been close to us for many years. She was as pure as they come. I did not know the groom's parents and asked her about their background.

"Tell me a little about Anthony," I asked Emma.

She answered, "Anthony's parents were divorced and each remarried about fifteen years ago. His mom, Catherine, took quite a *chunk of change* from the divorce and was remarried to a man she met in Essex while on vacation. Her husband had no family, so when he died, Catherine received his sizeable estate.

"Catherine is in her late seventies, and her health is not good," she added. "When she dies, the remaining estate from his mom will pass to Anthony and his sisters. He already has bought a home in the suburbs where we intend to live until his mom dies. Then we plan on purchasing a bigger home with more room for a family."

It was hard for me to find words. This young beautiful bride-to-be was always so sweet and well mannered, and yet she spoke of her mother-in-law's death like it was part of a family business plan. Because it was! It was paralyzing to hear her answer to my question, "Tell me about Anthony." But she wasn't finished.

"Anthony's dad, Chris, also remarried. He and his wife get along fair, so his dad has been careful to segregate the estate to go only to Anthony and his siblings. He has provided a life insurance policy for his wife to keep her happy so there will be no arguments. Chris is also not in the best of health. His wife constantly cajoles him to include her in a greater portion of the estate, but the siblings are always there to keep an eye on her."

Emma was on a roll and continued, "When Anthony's dad dies, one-third of the estate drops right in Anthony's lap. We think that will happen in the next five years, so we are going to wait to have children in case we decide to move to another state to raise our family. Anthony would no longer be dependent on practicing law to earn our family's living." It was clear Anthony and his siblings believed they had a right to expect to benefit from his parents' divorce and eventual death.

Keep in mind this little conversation was the day before Emma's wedding. Is your first reaction that this was inappropriate and entitled behavior? There is little question you are right. It shouldn't be surprising. Entitled behavior in children typically originates with a parent who makes the decision to share estate or financial information with their children. The excuse I hear most often is, "We want them to be prepared and have a plan for what to do if something happens to Mom and Dad unexpectedly."

> *Entitled behavior in children typically originates with a parent who makes the decision to share estate or financial information with their children.*

Many wealthy parents engage specialty firms that offer seminars that attempt to train children on how to receive massive transfers of wealth. Many of my own family clients have participated in these seminars. Success is the exception, not the rule. These courses are taught by nonwealthy businesspeople and educators who rarely have had the experience of inheriting wealth. Wealth, of any portion, must be managed for the most part by the parent, and they must leave plans in place that help manage the money even after they have passed.

Conspiracy Replaces Concern

When Mom and Dad begin to age, children who have been invited to influence Mom and Dad's estate plan often take an unhealthy attitude toward their parents' health. Sons and daughters begin to discuss their parents' health and competency behind their backs. It is a conspiracy—always in the name of "what's best for Mom and Dad"—but still a conspiracy. "Don't you think Dad is getting a little forgetful?" "Isn't Mom walking and talking a little more slowly?" "When do you think we should step in and insist Mom and Dad turn over the financial responsibility to the children?" Notice they are less concerned with aiding Mom and Dad with their physical and mental condition. The lack of financial responsibility could cause a loss of the money . . . which eventually belongs to them! So why not take over the bank accounts now? "*We* can decide what Mom and Dad need from here on out." The children may be more interested in the *estate* of their parents' health rather than the *state* of their health.

One adult "child" client of mine witnessed his mom and dad (each over eighty years old) invest in deals that eventually lost a lot of money. The parents were not as sharp as they had been in the days when the original money was made. It was painful for their adult children to watch this. Even I recommended the sons and daughter take over. But the kids (in their fifties) wanted to honor their parents. It was about dignity. It was *their* money. It was both painful and inspiring to witness. It is also very counterintuitive. Why would you let a vacuum cleaner salesman take $1,000 from your mom? You might not. But how can you avoid it in a way that puts Mom's dignity first?

Also, if you have money, recognize that your children will most likely be at war when you die. They won't fight over your memory. They will fight over your money. It doesn't take millions. It has happened over an estate of $200,000. Mom and Dad, the lifetime buffer between the children, will be gone. Sometimes you would not recognize your own children. Many will act out behavior they have been storing for an entire lifetime. The estranged brother will instantly become the financial expert when demanding something from Mom and Dad's estate. Many of your family members will never speak to one another again.

Your Fortune or Your Family

In planning your exit, make things as automatic as possible. Give clear instructions. Sell everything, pay whatever tax you must, and give them the proceeds, leaving no argument. Don't leave your home, or vacation home, or boat, or company to all of your kids. You will be injecting a virus into your lineage.

I can hear the objections. "We have our whole family working in our company. They get along fine." It is temporary. And there is resentment in one or more siblings already. They just won't tell you. When you put forward your son as the CEO on your death, and give the CEO the option to buy the others out at a prearranged stock price, the remaining kids will feel you placed them at a continuing auction with their oldest brother being the only bidder and with them as the merchandise. Ask yourself what you consider most important—the happiness of your kids or the continuation of the company and fortune you built? Try not to lie to yourself. Clients pass away. And soon after is often when everyone else's behavior changes. Children of entitlement do not develop overnight. But the death of a parent can bring them into full bloom.

Matthew was a longtime client. He had two sons: Matthew Jr. and Jasper. After Matthew Sr. lost his wife to ovarian cancer, he did his best to maintain a relatively modest lifestyle. His communication with his two boys was very intentional. They were educated and didn't appear to deviate from the norm any more than average growing kids. But as Matthew Jr. reached his thirties, he witnessed the attention that accompanied wealth. And because he didn't originate the wealth, those around him paid him respect but with little sincerity.

Kids of wealthy families have to be extraordinarily careful in their demeanor, because most people are watching for character flaws out of jealousy and hoping to see something they can gossip about. In the world of romance, Matthew Jr. soon realized the women who were attracted to him wanted to have a good time, and because Matthew Jr. was inclined to show off his money to get attention, women noticed. The women who lined up were less than long term.

Matthew Sr. died suddenly of pancreatic cancer when he was sixty-five. It was caught in the later stages, so he only lived six weeks past the diagnosis. The funeral was in Paso Robles at their ranch. People came from hundreds of miles away, and the funeral took on the character of a spiritual celebration. It was a great honor for Matthew Sr. At the funeral portion of the day, Matthew Jr. walked up to me, and for the first time referenced his father by his first name, "Matthew" rather than "Dad." He calmly asked, "By the way, do you know where the keys are to Matthew's motocross bike? I want to take it out this weekend." There wasn't time to respond before the ceremony began.

At the reception, Matthew Jr. saw me across the room and motioned to get my attention. His girlfriend was sitting in the chair next to him. When I came over to him, he put his finger on my chest, looked at her, and right in front of her said, "I want you to go ahead and draft the prenuptial agreement. It's probably about time to get on with life."

His girlfriend looked up at him and, stumbling to find words, asked, "Are you proposing to me?"

"Yeah, and you can go pick out a ring at Tiffany's tomorrow. Just keep it under four carats!" She stood up suddenly in tears and embraced Matthew Jr. The proposal was over, a wedding would be planned. I'm not even sure I heard her say "Yes."

How could Matthew Sr. have done better? Probably by simply telling his sons that when he died, others would take care of the family wealth, and the boys would not be permitted to allow the money to change their current lifestyles. Matthew Sr. should have told his sons that the majority of assets would be managed for profit and would not become a treasure chest of toys for the boys to spoil themselves and their families with.

Wealth should be a security blanket for your children, not a shroud. After witnessing and being involved in countless estates after Mom and Dad pass away, one thing is clear: The legal system and eager children have no problem getting to your money. And within a matter of weeks, the process of mourning your loss, and accessing an enhanced lifestyle utilizing your wealth, are processed in two separate parts of your child's brain. The money is no longer yours, but theirs. If the estate is so large that the adult "child" doesn't have the experience to manage the assets, you are best served by hiring a professional trustee, or your CPA, to administer the trust.

> **Wealth should be a security blanket for your children, not a shroud.**

———

Don't familiarize your children with their upcoming lifestyle perks. They might begin to look forward to it!

CHAPTER 13

DON'T Hand Down Too Much

"SAVING IS A GOOD IDEA . . .
ESPECIALLY WHEN IT IS DONE BY PARENTS."
—Winston Churchill

NO MATTER HOW MUCH LIFE WISDOM YOU HAVE ACQUIRED, NO matter how positive and heartfelt your intentions are, you can—unknowingly—hurt the generations after you if you bequeath too much money.

Parents of means typically grapple with the question, *How much should I leave my children?* Many want their children to have what they didn't have. Deciding how to hand down your estate is the last act of significant parental control, but it often carries an unexpected impact.

Many parents can't spend their own money during their lifetime because it is tied up in the ownership of a home, kept carefully in savings, or is a death benefit in a life insurance policy. It is a tree the parents planted, cultivated, watered, nurtured, and sacrificed to grow . . . yet the children get the fruit. Sounds typical, doesn't it? In fact, if *you* have been lucky enough to own your home and acquire a little savings, your daughters and sons are set to receive that money, right?

Develop Inheritance Insurance

Before you carry through with your fait accompli, consider this carefully. All people have needs and wants. Money, without out carefully drafted instructions and guidelines, can transform wants into needs. Rarely do you hear about people using their inherited money to pay down their mortgage, to nestle it away for their financial security, or to donate money to their church's hunger-relief project. More often you hear about adult children indulging in extravagances and blowing their inheritance to satisfy frivolous desires.

> **Money, without carefully drafted instructions and guidelines, can transform wants into needs.**

If you and your spouse happen to die suddenly and your children are still minors or young adults, imagine the results of handing one of your kids $100,000 today. What result would you expect? Remember, if you die with or without a will, the money goes to your child at either eighteen or twenty-one years of age depending on the state. Although a living trust has the option of a delayed payout, most parents give their children the inheritance at twenty-five or thirty years of age. Recall when *you* were twenty-five and what your thought process might have been if someone gave you a house worth $500,000, $100,000 in cash, and perhaps a couple of late-model automobiles. Someone at the

age of eighteen or twenty-five doesn't have the maturity to manage this amount of inherited wealth.

Think about the minimum-wage job you had as a young adult,
working your way toward college or graduate school. I'm betting
a windfall of unexpected cash might have made the call of the
highway tempting. The more significant the inheritance, the less
likely it is your children will ever return to the journey they were
previously on to find their true passion.

The prospect of an inheritance can bring on ugly behavior. I
thought I had seen it all, but even I was shocked by what trans-
pired at the funeral mass for my client Alex, a great, self-made
man who died three months after he was diagnosed with brain
cancer. While the priest was giving the Eucharist, and many people were weeping, his eldest son, Brent, a Tulane communica-
tions graduate, looked over and made eye contact with me. He
had always been very respectful of my position as consigliere and
legal advisor of the family and just as happy to comply with his
father's wishes during his life. When Brent finally caught my
glance, he pointed at me, and then with his index and middle
fingers pointed at his own eyes, and then directed his fingers at
me again, then back to his own eyes with two fingers. He then
pointed at his watch as if to convey urgency. I was baffled. It
had to be a gesture of compassion, or so I thought. It was a little
annoying he had anything on his mind other than his father, who
lay ten feet away . . . in a box.

After the ceremony, Brent made his way through the crowd
of roughly five hundred people and walked directly to me. This
is typically when family members of one of my clients would
tell me how much I meant to the deceased and how much they
depended on my guidance and advice. As Brent approached, he
began the same gesture of pointing at me with his two fingers

and then over his own eyes. When he was an arm's length in front of me he spoke. "You and I are going to be connected at the hip." The pointing eye gesture was about us seeing eye-to-eye.

His next comment caught me off guard. Pointing at his watch again, he said, "You and I are going to need to get together and *round up the ponies on Alex's estate.*" For a moment, I looked over my right shoulder because I thought Brent was talking to someone else. The family had no connection with horses or ponies, and Brent's tone was demanding, when his father had always addressed me with respect.

"Are you available at 8:00 a.m. on Monday?" Brent insisted.

"To do what?" I asked.

"I need to know exactly how much money Alex left the 'stepmonster' and who gets the beach house. I want to deep-six Jim (Alex's longtime money manager from Wells Fargo) and give the money to my bud who just started his own money management gig."

Brent wasn't even making eye contact with me now. There was so much disrespect spun into one mouthful, it took me a moment to hunt for my response. In fact, I was actually counting how many people he was able to insult in one comment—his stepmother; his father; his family financial advisor; and by his timing, just about every person at the service. But make no mistake, the person primarily at fault for Brent's behavior couldn't hear it. He was dead.

Most parents are unwilling to admit responsibility for their entitled children. They believe somehow their children had "choices" and could have "chosen" not to take their station in life and material possessions for granted. These parents are sincere in their belief. They don't see their child changing from day to day. Yet, the parent is primarily in charge of this incredible labor of love. It is up to you to teach your children to value you and respect what you have created.

Leaving Less Leaves More

Alex contributed to Brent's worldview—"Greed is good"—by giving too much financial support while he was alive and by neglecting to plan carefully regarding the disposition of his estate. If you want to prevent entitlement in your children, I would suggest you change the question most parents ask when they consider what to leave to their children.

Don't ask yourself, "How much money is too much to give my children?" Instead, ask a bolder question: "How much money is too little to leave my children?"

> **"How much money is too little to leave my children?"**

You're offended, right? You earned this, and you are certain your kids are different from others. Maybe. But probably not. Consider allowing your child to determine his or her own lifestyle and be responsible for financing that lifestyle. Suppose you give them no financial assistance in life other than basic food, shelter, and clothing.

Guess what? You would now be joining ninety-eight percent of Americans and ninety-nine percent of the free world. When my clients approach me to discuss how to maximize passing their wealth to their children, my canned response is to have them mull over the idea of leaving their kids nothing and, next, to carefully consider and write down what negative effects giving them no money may have.

Their first reaction is always astonishment and horror at the thought of the waste. Parents work and struggle their whole lives to provide a nest egg for themselves, and then at death, they plan to provide a mini lotto—unearned money—to their family. Mom and Dad see this gesture as providing security for their kids after they are gone. But does it really? Do you see only benefits and security resulting from your children having access to more money than they earned? What if you were to learn that seventy percent of the people who land sudden windfalls lose that money in several years?

In my thirty-three years of advising families, some extremely wealthy and some just passing on the value of their homes, unforeseen negative consequences have been the rule more than the exception. The children who inherit have experienced temporary euphoria followed by upset, anxiety, anger, depression, divorce, family separation, and sibling wars. Death and money bring out the worst in family relations.

Consider that building wealth is like building a dam. You build it across a river of opportunity to create a lake of your own success. Yours may be a small dam across a stream, or a large dam fording a river. A lake of wealth begins to form behind the dam. But watching the water trickle or rush into your lake, and watching it grow, is satisfying and rewarding . . . *for you.*

Now imagine that the generations who follow you are living downstream of your dam. Notice that all streams downstream of a dam generally flow at a lesser volume than the stream entering the dam. The flow is controlled by you, the dam operator. The quality of life for the inhabitants downstream is typically dependent on the amount of water released over or through the dam.

If you shut off the water completely, your kids would have to go elsewhere to survive and perhaps create their own dam. But kids don't really know the difference, so they will live down-stream and accept the flow determined by Mom and Dad. If a constant flow of water is released, they will have a green valley and set up their lives as close to the water flow as possible. If the water flow increases moderately, the flow downstream will increase, and they will simply move back away from the river but still stay as close as they can get. The children still don't comprehend anything upstream. They don't know dam build-ing, and they don't experience managing the water level in the lake. They just live, dependent on the water being supplied by someone else.

Dam breaks are catastrophic and generally destroy everything downstream. Think of your best-intended benevolence toward your kids as a dam break. Allowing wealth of any measure to be released downstream without careful thought may destroy an entire generation of your family. The more wealth you have, the further downstream your wealth can reach.

Will Your Wallet Be Your Legacy?

So let's suppose you leave nothing to your kids. If that both-ers you, then you have to ask yourself whether your kids are self-supporting. If they're not, why not? If you have one child who graduated college and is a dentist and another who has moved from one job to the next barely scratching out a living, why isn't it okay for the second child to continue as he wishes and to live as he is able to provide for himself? Oh, it's a girl? So that makes her more vulnerable and justifies enabling? We have a woman in her forties in Laguna Beach who pushes a shopping cart around town and sleeps in the park. Call her vulnerable;

she wouldn't care. Try to take her shopping cart, and she will scratch your eyes out. People toughen to the degree required by their circumstance.

If that still makes you feel uneasy, have you been financially supporting her? For how long? Put a simple word on that process: enabling. Did your child decide she was unhappy with the lifestyle she was experiencing, or did you? Again, enabling. Now you are feeling really uneasy. Why don't you leave her alone and let her experience her own path? "Because I can't let her crash," you say. Be honest, *you* couldn't let *yourself* crash. The truth is we can't handle the truth. We, as parents, so desperately want to be successful that we let our own wants override common sense. We are afraid to let our children struggle.

If you believe when you are gone that your kids will sit back in a moment of meditative pause and feel gratitude to Mom and Dad each time they use a bit of their inheritance to buy a car, a new big-screen LCD, or a vacation home, then you are delusional. In over three decades of witnessing good families pass on money to their children, I have seen that it only takes one to three months for the child who inherited to forget Mom and Dad had anything to do with the source of their newly acquired good fortune.

If you are close to your children, they will grieve for you whether or not you leave them money. It will not bring you extra favor in their minds. Remember, too, that people in the community are nosy. They know who paid for the new sports car. Even if your child forgets where the money came from, people in the community won't. The more you leave to your children, the greater the chance that people in the community will think less of your children. Our nation has a history of rejecting kings and queens. Ninety-nine percent of us are still serfs. Money doesn't make you a lord, unless you made it yourself.

Think "Security Blanket"

What is the alternative? Consider this creative and relatively successful estate plan designed by a man who lived throughout the
second half of the twentieth century and amassed hundreds of
millions of dollars. He left much of his fortune to fund the construction of one of the country's most prestigious colleges. He
pushed the remainder downstream in a most ingenious way. He
offered the following proposal to his children, grandchildren, and
any great-grandchildren that might come. He set up his trust so
the money would not become available to any of his beneficiaries until they reached the age of sixty. At that age, he said, they
could retire and take an annual salary for the rest of their lives
equal to the salary each had averaged over the last three years
prior to retirement. For instance, if the beneficiary was a nurse
making $75,000 a year, he or she would receive a nurse's pay. But
if he or she were the CEO of a publicly traded company making
$750,000 a year, he or she would get that salary. He thought it
wise to offer his kin a relaxed retirement at the income level they
had achieved during their careers. He also offered an additional
carrot. He said that if any of his beneficiaries were to devote their
retirement years to a nonprofit of their choice, his trust would
make an annual $1 million donation to that organization.

This parent was thinking. His plan called for productivity as
a measure of continued compensation, donating time to a wor-
thy cause with financial support for that cause, or the continuation of a lifestyle that was the equivalent of that experienced
prior to turning sixty years old. But you say, "I don't have millions
of dollars to give away." Well, what if you put together a trust
that provided for splitting the educational costs of your future
grandchildren between the trust and their parents? What if you
offered a stipend of $500 a month after age sixty to any of your

children as long as they are employed full time for the preceding five years? Be creative. Think security blanket, not windfall.

Estate planning attorneys, despite their best intentions, have one directive—to minimize estate taxes so your children net as much money as is legal. Are they experienced with or concerned about what happens next? Ask them what they think about children inheriting significant sums of money, and their answer will convince you they rarely give the question much thought.

Your last will and testament, or family trust, should carry a warning:

> **TAKING MONEY FROM THIS WILL OR TRUST** may have toxic consequences including a sudden change in lifestyle, a mania to shop, sibling family disputes, arguments with your spouse, a loss of motivation, alienation from good friends, a swarming of wealth professionals and professional fundraisers, a reacquaintance with distant family, and a mailbox full of catalogs.

The secret to preventing a sense of entitlement in your children after you die is to avoid changing the lifestyle of your children. Let your son or daughter's family live at the financial level they have acquired and earned. If they are teachers, allow them to continue as teachers. If they are struggling, let them continue to struggle until they decide to do something about it. If they are destitute, permit them basic needs of life. If they are addicts or alcoholics, don't try to micromanage what they themselves cannot easily change. Afford them the pathway to rehabilitation if, and when, they decide it is time. Money can be a comfort if it acts as a safety net and is not used to increase your child's station in life.

Start with the premise your children need only inherit family memories— good or bad—but no money! Now remember *your* circumstance at various times in your life: starting a new family, buying a house, or shopping for a new car. What effect would unearned money have had on those historical circumstances? Now consider whether money would benefit your children in the same or similar instance. Your answer in most cases should be "No." Ask how you would best provide a security blanket rather than a blank check.

> *Money is like a narcotic: a little more is always welcome, and the last amount never quite fills your present need.*

Also, never give money directly to your grandchildren. You are unwise to take parenting away from parents.

One tool that can be very helpful is to invest at least part of the inheritance in the form of a nonprofit family entity such as a private foundation, donor advised fund, or charity. For some of these funds, there is no set-up charge, no charge to administrate, and you will receive a modest rate of return on your money. Account minimum? $1,000! Allow your adult children to be codirectors of that family enterprise and determine where the money can be donated. Stipulate that the money is not for the use of family members. The adult children who decide to participate will have the opportunity to discover good causes and worthwhile people or organizations in need of financial support and to give away money on behalf of your family.

That will be gratifying and will build family relations long after you are gone. Your family will be remembered for its generosity. You will be remembered for being wise and intentional with your money.

———

Although it may be difficult to consider leaving your children only a modest amount of money, perhaps it is your last act of "tough love." Don't turn a blind eye to the reality that even modest amounts of money carelessly given can have unexpected and corrupting results. Money is like a narcotic: a little more is always welcome, and the last amount never quite fills your present need. Give your children enough that they do something but not so much they do nothing. Your legacy, and perhaps theirs, is in your hands.

Give your children enough that they do something but not so much they do nothing.

For Everything You Give Your Child, You Take Something Away

IT IS COUNTERINTUITIVE *NOT* TO GIVE TO OUR CHILDREN. WE parents believe giving is a good thing. But how much giving is too much to give our children? When do we lose the balance and awareness that the uniqueness of our children will never emerge if we continue to provide them with the answers to problems they need to solve themselves, or work overtime to shield them from life's struggles?

Parents, at all income levels, are captive to the fiction that it is their responsibility to take away the struggle in their children's lives. Most parents dream their children will have better lives than they do. In recent times, "a better life" *For everything you give your child, you take something away.* has become defined primarily by financial stability, but often in assisting children, parents dull the character, integrity, work ethic, and socialization skills their children need to become responsible and independent adults.

The responsible and intentional parent makes an effort to contemplate, discuss, and if possible determine what life lessons will be missed if failure is averted and financial support is offered. A responsible and intentional parent guards against becoming codependent and micromanaging their children's lives and works hard to stay emotionally healthy themselves.

Your teenager gets a DUI while driving intoxicated. Do you run to your IRA and mortgage your own retirement to bail him out of jail, hire the best lawyer, and then start listening and believing the lawyer's contrived rationalizations of how legal technicalities such as body weight and lack of food intake should excuse the five beers he downed before jumping behind the wheel of a car? Maybe you should leave him in jail for the night or allow him to experience the consequences of his actions.

"What?" you say, "My child? He is an honor student and superstar athlete!" So what? He was also irresponsible and a danger to innocent people on the highway. What lesson do you want to teach—that bad and dangerous behavior is excusable if you can afford to sidestep the law? Or do you want your son and daughter to think twice the next time they drink and sit behind the wheel of an automobile? If your teenager had injured someone in an accident, he would be on his way to prison for an extended term.

Make no mistake, the development of entitlement in a child is exclusively the fault of the parent. In the name of protecting their children, parents create a literal disconnect between the real world and the safe and ideal world in which they would have their children live. Children don't have their own built-in warning light to alert them to entitlement approaching. They have no foundation to know they are taking their privileges for granted. We parents have cleared the struggles from the pathway to success *for* them. We teach them they are entitled to have everything they want. When no earning or learning takes place between acquiring one material thing and the next, purchasing a new car feels no more satisfying to them than purchasing a new bicycle. Value escapes. There is a richness missing from their lives.

Michelangelo hammered on the marble block until *David* escaped. Too many parents fear the pain that will come when life's struggles beat down on their children, but these are the very experiences that mold and shape their children's character and passions so those children may escape and become adults— unique works of art.

It is normal to experience a life filled with repeated fluctuations, with ups and downs, with trying and difficult times— followed by periods of satisfaction and contentment. Difficult times loom momentarily but eventually recede and allow us to move forward again. We learn. Hard times cause us to struggle internally with our own egos, ambitions, sense of personal worth, societal position, self-image, concerns about how others perceive us, health, addictions, failings, sense of financial stability, and our spirituality.

And if that isn't enough, the outside world joins in to add to the storm. We get fired; lose our home to foreclosure; lose a parent, spouse, or child; file for divorce; get a traffic ticket; our car breaks down; or we have a good friend disappoint us. But we learn to press on. And when the clouds of hardship and struggle clear, we feel grateful and proud and, for a while, content. Sometimes it is enough just to have calm. Welcome to the hills and valleys of life. You cannot avoid these rhythms of life at any income level. They find everyone.

Many parents incessantly attempt

> *There is nothing better for children than to crash and burn as a result of their own errors in judgment and mistakes and for them to experience the consequences of their choices.*

(and often succeed) to make their children's lives easier and less taxing than their own. Such parental ethics are either well-intentioned errors or just plain laziness. There is nothing better for children than to crash and burn as a result of their own errors in judgment and mistakes and for them to experience the consequences of their choices. You can tell a child not to put her hand on a hot stove ten times without success. It only takes letting her insist on it once for the child to learn the lesson.

So spend at least a little time looking at the downside of your support. Remember: *for everything you give your child, you take something away.* Before you "take away the pain" of your children's struggle or misfortune, consider what benefit they might receive from your willingness to listen, love, discuss, and console in lieu of handing over your wallet for the solution. It is ironic how we hope to help our children avoid the same toil that gives *us* so much satisfaction to overcome. We endured . . . and so will they . . . IF we let them.

Index

About the Author

Photograph by David Lebon

As personal advisor and legal counsel to the super wealthy, Richard Watts is called on to counsel his clients on some of the most intimate decisions they have to make. He spends his workdays within the castle walls of America's most successful families.

Richard studied economics at University of California at San Diego, Earl Warren College, and was admitted to practice law in California in 1982. He is an alumnus of Harvard Business School.

His primary passion is conveying the wisdoms of life through his practice, lectures, and writings.

Richard and his wife, Debbie, live in Laguna Beach, California, in the neighborhood of their three boys: Aaron, Todd, and Russell; two daughters by marriage, Rene and Stephanie; and their four extra-special grandchildren, Maclane, Lucy, Chandler, and Bennett.

You can also find Richard surfing at San Onofre, golfing at Santa Ana Country Club, or sitting in a local coffee shop with friends, talking about subjects that really matter.